god is Love

god is love

ESSAYS FROM PORTLAND MAGAZINE

EDITED BY BRIAN DOYLE

Augsburg Books
MINNEAPOLIS

GOD IS LOVE
Essays from Portland Magazine

Large-quantity purchases or custom editions of this book are available at a discount from the publisher. For more information, contact the sales department at Augsburg Fortress, Publishers, 1-800-328-4648, or write to: Sales Director, Augsburg Fortress, Publishers, P.O. Box 1209, Minneapolis, MN 55440-1209.

Book design by Michelle L. N. Cook
Cover design by Jessica A. Klein; cover art by Norman Laliberté

ISBN 0-8066-4449-4

The copyright page continues on page 139.

The paper used in this publication meets the minimum requirements of American National Standard for Information Sciences—Permanence of Paper for Printed Library Materials, ANSI Z329.48-1984. ♾ ™

Manufactured in the U.S.A.

07   06   05   04   03   1   2   3   4   5   6   7   8   9   10

Dedication

To the University of Portland's genius typesetter, Susan Säfve, who not only typeset every one of these essays to appear in the University of Portland's *Portland Magazine,* but commented freely, intelligently, tartly on them to the editor, and so added to the magazine not only the grace of her compositional art, but the considerable wit and substance of her heart.

Contents

INTRODUCTION 1

BEN BIRNBAUM / *Why I Pray* 5
ANNIE CALLAN / *The Ambulance Prayer* 7
JOHN DANIEL / *Holy Waters* 8
BRIAN DOYLE / *Leap*. 16
ANDRE DUBUS / *Making Sandwiches for My Daughters* 18
DAVID JAMES DUNCAN / *Gladly* 24
MARY GORDON / *Six Prayers*. 29
TONY HILLERMAN / *Offer It Up*. 33
BARRY LOPEZ / *God's Love on a Darkling Plain* 36
MELISSA MADENSKI / *Breathless* 39
LOUIS MASSON / *Holy Places, Holy People* 43
GREGORY MCNAMEE / *Spiritual Peaks* 50
KATHLEEN DEAN MOORE / *Baking Bread with My Daughter* 58
CYNTHIA OZICK / *Love Is What We Do* 61
CHET RAYMO / *The Meadow*. 64
PATTIANN ROGERS / *Rain*. 68
PATTIANN ROGERS / *Where God's Grief Appears*. 73
MARY LEE SETTLE / *One Clear Chord*. 75
BISHOP WILLIAM SKYLSTAD / *The Waters of Life* 78
KIM STAFFORD / *Spirit-Homesteading the Oregon Country* 83
MARGARET STEINFELS / *Religion vs. the Media* 92
SALLIE TISDALE / *Grace*. 95
MARGARET VISSER / *The Geometry of Love* 101
ARCHBISHOP JOHN VLAZNY / *Dreaming God's Dream* 115
TERRY TEMPEST WILLIAMS / *Santa Teresa*. 117
EDWARD O. WILSON / *Making Religion* 124

NOTES ON THE CONTRIBUTORS. 134

Introduction

A MAGAZINE IS A CURIOUS BEAST. IT BEGINS AS A STEW OF IDEAS, lurches through the byzantine wanderings of many minds, becomes eventually a hill of manuscripts and galley proofs and paintings and photographs and drawings. Then it is for a brief time held completely on a computer disk, and then it becomes thousands of proof sheets at the printer, and then, as if by magic, it is a magazine, launched through the mails toward the desks, settees, bathrooms, dens, bedrooms, porches, and couches of its readers—in *Portland Magazine*'s case, readers in fifty states and forty nations around the world. Portable, beautiful, opinionated, informative, and weighing about eight ounces, it is a quarterly collection of stories and voices and faces that is designed and built to stimulate the minds and hearts of its readers.

An interested scholar of magazines might trace *Portland Magazine*'s origins to the University of Portland's very first periodical, *The Columbiad*, a (very good) student magazine first published in 1903, but *Portland* in its current form began in 1984, under John Soisson, its first editor. John wanted to make a magazine of substance: he felt that the very best way to advance the work and ideas of the University of Portland was to collect and tell its most revelatory and substantive stories in a periodical that would be credible, attractive, and thought-provoking—something more complex and honest than the usual alumni magazine, yet something that would in each of its parts gently tell an aspect of the University of Portland's particular story.

As the University was and is Catholic, headquartered in the vast beauty of the Pacific Northwest, devoted primarily to fine teaching, and particularly sensitive to the personal touch in its classes, life, and rhetoric, its magazine too would be deeply interested in religion and spirituality, in the nature and character of this region, and in "the inarticulate speech of the heart," as the great Irish composer and poet Van Morrison sings.

Soisson invented and ran a *Portland* that quickly became, according to the international Council for the Advancement and Support of Education, one of the ten best university magazines in the nation during his tenure, 1984-1990. His successor, the undersigned, has for twelve years now tried to make a quarterly *Portland Magazine* that would be as enlightening and educational, as revelatory of the University's stories and character and work and ideas and people, but also one that would also occasionally be riveting, startling, extraordinary, and—in the words of one perceptive reader—"vulnerable to emotion." *Portland Magazine* has carried some astonishing work in its pages, very often writing of great spiritual discernment and honesty, and the best of those essays are collected here.

Perhaps magazine editors are like basketball coaches, in that they receive a little too much credit for the quality of the effort they direct. So I take this opportunity to publicly thank a number of men and women who have worked hard and long to make *Portland Magazine* an extraordinary creature. They are:

Portland's obviously brilliant publisher from 1990-2003, University of Portland president Father David Tyson, C.S.C.;

its talented and patient art director and *de facto* associate editor from 1984-2003, Joseph Erceg;

the brusque and honest University vice president who found the money for *Portland* annually (and gave the editor the freedom that results in a terrific magazine), Tony DiSpigno;

its assistant editors from 1984-2003, the late Bob Boehmer, Teri Cettina, Sarah Bleeg, John Ferris, Christine Fundak Rohan, Amy Harrington, and Marc Covert;

its personable contributing editor, University literature professor Louis Masson, who has written the magazine's "Reflections" column for fifteen years (his essays from *Portland* have been collected in the book *Reflections: Essays of Place and Family*), and who is invaluable to the editor for his dark humor;

its genius typesetter, Susan Säfve, who so often acts as first reader and editorial commentator;

its able mailing queen, the smiling and efficient Gayle Alderman;

and the men who have overseen its actual publication for fifteen years, often in the deep blue reaches of the night, poring over proofs as the presses hammered loudly in their ears, the smiling and efficient Jim Spring and Ron Brown of Bridgetown Printing Company in Portland, Oregon.

Thanks also, heartfelt and hearty, to all the artists and writers who have literally composed the magazine over the years: You have graced the magazine and the University. And to the many men and women (and children) who have offered ideas, both politely and apoplectically, to the editor, muttered thanks.

And final thanks to the people for whom the magazine is made, to whom the editorial essays are addressed, who write and call and e-mail and fax me with their firm and so often penetrating opinions:

the magazine's 30,000 readers.

Bless you.

—Brian Doyle

Why I Pray

BEN BIRNBAUM

I ONCE SAW GOD. I AM NOT SURE WHETHER *SAW* IS THE RIGHT word, or *God*, for that matter, but those are the words I have.

I was a six-year-old boy standing alone at the bottom of a sloped meadow about 120 miles northwest of my home in New York City. Above the meadow were wooded mountains, and above that a clear sky.

My father had brought us from the city to a hotel near that meadow for two weeks of summer, and even if I hadn't run into God that afternoon, I would remember those days because they marked the first time I entered a hotel, was served by a waiter, and was stung by a bee.

It was a kosher and Sabbath-observant hotel, which I don't offer to explain why God was loitering nearby, but to signal that I came of a devout family (as did nearly every person I knew) and that I was well aware, even at that age, of who God was and what He had done to date.

What happened is difficult to explain. The world became radiant, though not the kind of radiant that makes you blink or close your eyes. In fact, it was not light that radiated (though it seemed light), but something more complex, something like a tone as it swells on the back of a chord that is being sounded by a full orchestra. As human perception goes, in fact, it might be most accurate to say that I felt as though something had called out and I had heard.

And hearing, I felt free, rooted, floating, flooded, ablaze, remote, close, certain, joyous, and—strangely, given the circumstances—absolutely calm. In the cavern of my chest, in the thin arms at my sides, inside the Keds that lightly pressed the soil, blood pulsed at a solid sixty-two beats per minute.

Given what I had been taught, I should not have thought that this was God—something wonderful, certainly, but not God. The God I knew, and even loved, commanded us, reproved us, made us attentive and busy. He was a Hebrew speaker, of course, but above all a speaker. Sound and light shows, tricks of transcendence, were not his racket (not in recent millennia anyway), nor was He known to spend a lot of time in the American woods. But I knew that this was God that I had seen or who had seen me, and I did not at the time think this remarkable, and for some reason still don't. It wasn't as if, for example, I had seen a bear or a deer come out of the woods and cross the meadow. That is something I would have related to my mother. About God I said nothing.

One afternoon, fifteen or so years later, I resigned from the rabbinical seminary I was attending. I went to the dean of students, a man with a long black beard and no visible sense of humor, and told him I was leaving, that I had lost my faith. He didn't express shock; he didn't try to convince me to stay on. What he said was: "But you still pray three times a day, right?"

Years later, long after I'd stopped being angry at his response, long after I'd stopped fretting about whether I believed, or why I believed, or if what I believed today was different from what I had believed last week, I read the transcript of a radio interview with Abraham Joshua Heschel in which he said, "Prayer may not save us. But it may make us worthy of being saved."

I pray so that I may be worthy: worthy of being saved (whatever that means), worthy of this miracle of days, worthy of my sadnesses, worthy of standing as a man and telling the story of that boy in blue jeans and Keds who came upon God in the sloping meadow and was not surprised.

The Ambulance Prayer

ANNIE CALLAN

EVER SINCE,
when I hear the siren call

I stop, midstride, midbite,
midword, and glide my palms
together at my chest.

Ever since,
I try to let them rest there
in response, *not dead, not dead*
and beg for blessings and
safe passage for today's
conveyance,

who just this morning
may have plucked the first lilac
off a bush—oh, sweet surprise—
and inhaled deeply of its promise
for a long, succulent summer.

Holy Waters

JOHN DANIEL

WE DON'T TEND TO ASK WHERE A LAKE COMES FROM: IT LIES before us, contained and complete, tantalizing in its depth but not its origin. A river is a different kind of mystery, a mystery of distance and source. Touch its fluent body and you touch far places. You touch a story that must end somewhere but will not stop telling itself, a story that is always just beginning.

The West Little Owyhee, the slight stream by which I've made my camp, starts somewhere in this vast sagebrush tableland of far southeastern Oregon, maybe in a pocket of aspens dropping leaves into a pool—and the pool stirs, trickling over stones. Stories begin that way throughout the high desert country, on Steens Mountain and Hart Mountain, in the Trout Creeks and the Ochocos. And they begin, too, in dry rocky creases that wander the immense landscape as if lost. They are not lost. When snow melts or enough rain falls they are the rivers gathering, finding their way, forming themselves as they gradually form the land.

In the Cascades and the Coast Range, the Wallowas and the Strawberries, there are other kinds of beginnings. Spotting the forests are seeps and springs where grasses, mosses, and horsetails silently riot, growing and dying to grow and die and grow again. There are lakes surrounded by conifers or alpine meadow, lakes brimming full and overfull, pouring off through little ravines checked with boulders and the trunks of trees and beaver dams.

Higher on the peaks there are slumping snow fields littered with rockfall and tinged with algae, the rubble below them glistening with melt. There are slow rivers of ice that hoard the story for centuries and let it go in minuscule drops, in streamings milky with ground stone.

Start at any of those sources, let water lead you, and eventually you will stand where a river empties into the Pacific or a desert lake. The story isn't hard to follow. But start at the mouth and trace the story back, and your journey may involve more questions. Trace the Rogue River, to choose one. From its outlet at Gold Beach on the southern coast, follow it back through its wild canyon in the Klamath Mountains, through its broad valley between Grants Pass and Medford, and up past Lost Creek Reservoir into the Cascades. Climb alongside through the volcanic landscape, where at one point the river hurls itself into a lava tube and churns out of sight for two hundred feet. Follow still higher, until the Rogue is nothing but a creek joined by other creeks, all issuing from mountain springs, all small and white and fast. You could follow any of them. *Here*, says the river, *here* and *here*.

Stay with the blue line your map calls the Rogue and you'll arrive at a place called Boundary Springs, high in the northwest corner of Crater Lake National Park. But even there you'll face choices. There are several springs, each of them bright with moss and rushing water. Where is the Rogue River now? The largest spring? Take off your boots, douse your feet. Watch how lucid water springs forth among shaggy stones and cascades lightly away. Watch how it flows. It does not gather and then begin to move. It is born in motion, a gesture already underway. This spring is the only place where a river emerges from the deep cold joints of an exploded mountain, a subterranean wilderness fed by seepings out of Crater Lake, which itself is fed by underground springs, which themselves are fed by snowmelt sinking into soil.

Snowfall, then, is the source of the Rogue. But snow is only an expression of winter storms, and the storms are swirling eddies of a vast air mass that flows out of Siberia, soaks up moisture south of the Aleutians, and delivers barrages of weather to our West Coast. It is known as the Pacific maritime polar airstream, one of seven such atmospheric tendencies that shape the North American climate. The headwaters of the Rogue, the headwaters of every stream on Earth, is a river in the sky.

NO ONE IN THE ANCIENT WORLD WOULD HAVE BEEN SURPRISED AT such an idea, but the ancients knew their rivers in the sky through myth, not atmospheric science. The early Greeks imagined a divine river as the god Oceanus, who encircled the universe and coupled with his wife and sister, Tethys, to produce the three thousand earthly rivers. The Egyptians believed that not one but two Niles flowed through their cosmos—the great river of water whose floods fertilized their fields, and a celestial Nile that rose from the same source and tended across the heavens. By day it bore the boat of Ra the Sun; at night it was visible as the Milky Way. As civilization evolved in the Ganges Valley of India, it was believed that a heavenly river identified with the goddess Shakti poured down upon the head of Shiva, who eased the torrential power of her waters and sent them streaming to the four directions. The southern branch became the River Ganges, which to Hindus is not only sacred but is divinity itself in liquid manifestation. Bathing in the Ganges, polluted as it may be, purifies one's present life—and past lives—of sin. Pilgrims take home bottles of its water for healing.

The Book of Genesis gives a brief glimpse of that same archetypal river: "And a river went out of Eden to water the garden; and from thence it was parted, and became into four heads." Almost all mythic cosmogonies begin with water. It is the primeval element, "the face of the deep," the formless potentiality that preexists the created world and sustains its being. "Water flows," wrote religious historian Mircea Eliade, "it inspires, it heals, it prophesies. By their very nature, spring and river display power, life, perpetual renewal; they *are* and they are *alive*."

In the Book of Jeremiah, God identifies his very being with that most precious of substances in an arid land: "They have forsaken me, the fountain of living waters." Ezekiel envisions the waters of life as a small trickle issuing from the threshold of the Jerusalem Temple. As the Lord leads him downstream, the waters rise to his ankles, his knees, his loins, and then they swell into a mighty river lined on both its banks with fruitful and medicinal trees. The image is echoed as the culminating vision of Revelation, in which the narrator is shown "a pure river of water of life, clear as crystal, proceeding out of the throne of God and of the Lamb."

In Greek mythology, the lively splash and stir of water came to be personified in the form of the nymphs, female divinities of birth and fertility who cured the sick and raised mortal children to be heroes. And, perhaps because water in motion seems to utter an elusive speech, oracles were often located near springs and streams. Before responding to questions, the oracle would drink from the waters, usually in a cave. Through him the mystery of living water expressed itself to the minds of human beings.

But like the oracle's news, the gifts of water were not always good. An ancient Syrian statue of the Great Mother shows her gowned in a river flowing from the vase she holds, fish swimming upward in its current. But the Goddess was also pictured with demonic eyes, lightning jagging from her brow. On the Nile, the Indus, the Tigris, and Euphrates, the giver of life was sometimes a destroyer, withholding her fertility and cancelling human lives through drought or flood. Even the nurturing nymphs were feared by the Greeks as thieves of children, and in the midday heat they were liable to emerge from rushing water in forms that could dissolve in madness any minds that beheld them. Through such images the ancients acknowledged that water is a wild power, ungovernable, containable only by paradox. Its nature is to create and to ruin, to sustain the things of creation and claim them to itself again.

THAT DUAL NATURE IS CENTRAL TO THE RITE OF BAPTISM, WHICH is at once a death—a disintegration of one's old identity—and a new birth, a pouring forth of the divine into one's mortal life. It was originally a ritual not simply of water but of flowing water, water in its living movement. In Egypt, purification by water was associated with Osiris and Isis, god and goddess of the rising and falling Nile. In Hindu tradition, water must be set in motion by pouring from a vessel when no stream or river is available. Among Jews before the time of Christ, baptism took place seven days after circumcision by immersing the naked child in a flowing stream. Ritual pools were used too, but John the Baptist shunned those and performed his baptisms in the River Jordan, long known for its healing power. It was in the Jordan that John baptized the mightier one who came after him—and when Jesus emerged from the river's current, "he saw the Spirit of God descending like a dove, and lighting upon him."

After Christ's death, baptism took on the added import of the Passion and the Resurrection: to give oneself to the water was to die with Christ, and to rise from it was to rise reborn through him. Many early Christians continued to baptize in John's way, as did Gnostic peoples such as the Mandaeans of Iran and Iraq. "Be baptized with the flowing water I have brought you from the world of light," it is written in their *Right Ginza*. "Clothe yourselves in white, to be like the mystery of this flowing water." In the modern world, pouring of water from a baptismal font or dunking in a pool are more common than immersion in a stream, but the symbolism of baptism remains powerful. Living water is the gesture from Beyond. It returns us to beginnings and makes us anew. It joins the timeless to the temporal, the sacred to the secular, the heavenly to the mundane.

But if flowing water is a thoroughfare between those realms, it is also—ever paradoxical—the line of demarcation between them. Perhaps because rivers, aside from seashores, form the clearest boundaries to be found in nature, the crossing of a river is the human psyche's primary symbol for the passage of death. Beyond the earthly Jordan lies the promised land; beyond the spiritual Jordan lies the promised land of heaven. The Greeks buried their dead with a coin in the mouth for Charon, the grumpy boatman who ferried souls across the River Acheron to the realms of Hades. The Babylonians had a similar notion, and the theme occurs in both the Shinto and Buddhist traditions of Japan—one of the ancient meanings of Nirvana is "the far shore." Among Hindus, holy sites are known as *tirthas*—fords—because they are considered propitious places to make the crossing from this earthly world of illusion. It was inevitable that Herman Hesse's Siddhartha should come to a river near the end of his life of seeking. He lived out his days as a ferryman, poling travelers on their necessary journeys as he meditated on the river, listened to its voices, and heard in it at last all laughter and all sorrow, the flowing wholeness he had yearned for his entire life.

GLANCING DOWN AT THE WILLAMETTE RIVER IN PORTLAND AS WE drive over the Broadway or Marquam or St. Johns bridges, we don't see it in mythic terms. We don't toss handfuls of grass as a sacrifice, as do the Masai of East Africa when they cross their rivers. Looking down from The Bluff on the workaday river with its tugs and tankers and ·dry docks, its riprapped banks, we aren't likely to think of it as sacred or alive, a gesture from another world. We aren't moved to perform baptisms in it. We of the modern age have sought other kinds of value in our rivers. We have subdued them and turned them into channels of commerce. We have diverted them to water our fields, loaded them with sewage, torn up their beds and banks for gold, blockaded them to control their floods and extract their energy, stripped and muddied their basins for timber and pasture, poisoned them with industrial waste, and reduced their abounding runs of anadromous fish to fractional remnants.

We have treated rivers as convenient perpetual motion machines, mere volumes of dutiful water at our disposal, yet even our tightly harnessed industrial rivers still beckon us. Whatever we have done to them, a mystery still flows before us. We walk and rest beside them, gazing, listening. When the docile waters rise, as they did in February of 1996, we flock to see the wildness in them, the wrack and foam, the intent sweeping power. Despite any damage floods do, it reassures us in our depths to know, with Wordsworth, that "The river glideth at his own sweet will."

All of us have touched and been touched by flowing water. Our ancestors have eaten and loved and raised children by rivers for as long as we have been human, and longer. We have known the various music of living water for the entire evolutionary saga of our coming of age on Earth. "It seems to flow through my very bones," wrote Thoreau of a brook he knew. "What is it I hear but the pure waterfalls within me, in the circulation of my blood, the streams that fall into my heart?"

Spiritually we understand rivers far less well than the ancients did, but even in the rational light of our science, the creative and destructive nature of running water remains wonderful enough. We know that it began its work as soon as rains first fell and traveled the face of the young volcanic planet, and if not for continual tectonic uplift, it would long ago have erased the continents into a global sea. Through that tireless attrition, that primordial youthful energy, water carves out runnels, clefts, ravines, hollows, valleys, chasms, canyons—the intricate inworn branching of watersheds, the aging face of the land, the very places we know as home. And in that webwork of water, in and around and gathered together by its flexuous body, a labyrinthine ecology connects our human lives to the least and greatest of the lives around us, an ecology we are only beginning to fathom and are unlikely ever to understand in its wholeness.

HISTORICALLY, RIVERS HAVE BEEN OUR CHIEF THOROUGHFARES OF exploration and settlement. They led us into the continent and eventually across it. They showed the way into the Oregon Country for Lewis and Clark, for the trappers and missionaries, for the pioneers of the Oregon Trail. Columbia, McKenzie, Illinois, John Day, Sprague, Smith, Deschutes, Powder, Malheur, Rogue—you can hear the history in the names, you can glimpse the stories we have spun around Oregon's rivers.

But listen to more: Klamath, Imnaha, Sycan, Umpqua, Elk, Salmon, Snake, Wenaha, Wallowa, Clackamas, Nestucca,

Chewaucan. There are other and older histories here, interwoven with the flowing of rivers for thousands of years before Europeans set foot on American land. And there are hints in those names of a truth beyond history or human culture, hints of a primeval vitality, hints of original voices sounding in the land before any human being was alive to listen.

The subdued autumnal music of the West Little Owyhee, flowing now in starlight beside the camp where I write, is one such voice, and there are many more. The Snake, where this mild water is bound, surges through Hells Canyon with the power of the Rocky Mountains behind it. The two Indian Creeks on Steens Mountain tumble down grassy, aspen-flagged valleys to the Donner und Blitzen ("Thunder and Lightning," so named by cavalry passing in an 1864 thunderstorm, and feeling romantic). The White River flings itself from Mount Hood's shoulders; the Metolius wends its stately way through ponderosa pines; the Chetco, rising in the rugged Kalmiopsis, incises steep-walled canyons down to the sea. Where we haven't restrained them, the rivers still sound, their fountains spring forth from the world of light, they pursue unhindered the blind and beautiful labor of time.

Anything in nature reflects the viewer, but of all the natural forms, rivers give back the fullest reflection of the human. They are lives in motion, bound up like ours in time and consequence, steadily being born and steadily dying. They stir in their sleep, they laugh and mourn, and—like us at our best—they are true to themselves under all conditions, changeful and changeless, free and constrained, a lively resurging presence of past and future made one. To seek a river's source is to seek our own, to turn and turn and always return—to snow and mountains, to sea and sky, and always to water, always to the soul's deep springs, always to the flowing ungraspable image that forever runs free of all names and knowing, singing the story of its own being, bearing forth from distant passages its mortal and infinite nature.

Leap

BRIAN DOYLE

A COUPLE LEAPED FROM THE SOUTH TOWER, HAND IN HAND. THEY reached for each other and their hands met and they jumped.

Many people jumped. Perhaps hundreds. No one knows. They struck the pavement with such force that there was a pink mist in the air.

The mayor reported the mist.

A kindergarten boy who saw people falling in flames told his teacher that the birds were on fire. She ran with him on her shoulders out of the ashes.

Several pedestrians were killed by people falling from the sky.

A fireman was killed by a body falling from the sky.

But a man reached for a woman's hand and she reached for his hand and they leaped out the window holding hands.

Jennifer Brickhouse of New Jersey and Stuart DeHann of New York City saw this from far below.

I try to whisper prayers for the sudden dead, and the harrowed families of the dead, and the screaming souls of the murderers, but I keep coming back to his hand and her hand nestled in each other with such extraordinary ordinary succinct ancient naked stunning perfect simple ferocious love.

It is the most powerful prayer I can imagine, the most eloquent, the most graceful. It is everything that we are capable of against horror and loss and death. It is what makes me believe that we are not craven fools and charlatans to believe in God, to believe that human beings have greatness and holiness within them like seeds that open only under great fires, to believe that some unimaginable essence of who we are persists past the dissolution of what we were, to believe against such evil evidence hourly that love is why we are here.

He that loveth his brother abideth in the light, wrote John the Apostle.

I trust I shall shortly see thee, and we shall speak face to face, John also wrote.

Jennifer Brickhouse saw them holding hands, and Stuart DeHann saw them holding hands, and I hold onto that.

Making Sandwiches for My Daughters

ANDRE DUBUS

A SACRAMENT IS PHYSICAL, AND WITHIN IT IS GOD'S LOVE; AS A sandwich is physical, and nutritious and pleasurable, and within it is love, if someone makes it for you and gives it to you with love; even harried or tired or impatient love, but with love's direction and concern, love's again and again wavering and distorted focus on goodness; then God's love too is in the sandwich.

A sacrament is an outward sign of God's love, they taught me when I was a boy, and in the Catholic Church there are seven. But, no, I say, for the Church is catholic, the world is catholic, and there are seven times seventy sacraments, to infinity. Today I sit at my desk in June in Massachusetts; a breeze from the southeast comes through the window behind me, touches me, and goes through the open glass door in front of me. The sky is blue, and cumulus clouds are motionless above green trees lit brightly by the sun shining in dry air. In humid air the leaves would be darkened, but now they are bright, and you can see lighted space between them, so that each leaf is distinct; and each leaf is receiving sacraments of light and air and water and earth. So am I, in the breeze on my skin, the air I breathe, the sky and earth and trees I look at.

Sacraments are myriad. It is good to be baptized, to confess and be reconciled, to receive Communion, to be confirmed, to be ordained a priest, to marry, or to be anointed with the sacrament of healing. But it is limiting to believe that sacraments occur only in churches, or when someone comes to us in a hospital or at home and anoints our brows and eyes and ears, our noses and lips, hearts and hands and feet. I need sacraments I can receive through my senses. I need God manifested as Christ, who ate and drank and shat and suffered; and laughed. So I can dance with Him as the leaf dances in the breeze under the sun.

Not remembering that we are always receiving sacraments is an isolation the leaves do not have to endure: They receive and give and they are green. Not remembering this is an isolation only the human soul has to endure. But the isolation of a human soul may be the cause of not remembering this. Between isolation and harmony, there is not always a vast distance. Sometimes it is a distance that can be traversed in a moment, by choosing to focus on the essence of what is occurring, rather than on its exterior: its difficulty or beauty, its demands or joy, peace or grief, passion or humor. This is not a matter of courage or discipline or will; it is a receptive condition.

BECAUSE I AM DIVORCED, ON TUESDAYS I DRIVE TO MY DAUGHTERS' school where they are in the seventh and second grades. I have them with me on other days, and some nights, but Tuesday is the school day. They do not like the food at their school, and the school does not allow them to bring food, so after classes they are hungry, and I bring them sandwiches, potato chips, Cokes, Reese's peanut butter cups. My kitchen is very small; if one person is standing in it, I cannot make a 360-degree turn. When I roll into the kitchen to make the girls' sandwiches, if I remember to stop at the first set of drawers on my right, just inside the door, and get plastic bags and write *Cadence* on one and *Madeline* on the other; then stop at the second set of drawers and get three knives for spreading mayonnaise and mustard and cutting the sandwiches in half; then turn sharply left and reach over the sink for the cutting board leaning upright behind the faucet; then put all these things on the counter to my right, beside the refrigerator, and bend forward and reach into the refrigerator for the meat and cheese and mustard and mayonnaise, and reach up into the freezer for bread, I can do all of this with one turn of the chair. This is a first-world problem; I ought to be only grateful. Sometimes I remember this, and then I believe that most biped fathers in the world would exchange their legs for my wheelchair and house and food, medical insurance and my daughters' school.

Making sandwiches while sitting in a wheelchair is not physically difficult. But it can be a spiritual trial; the chair always makes me remember my legs, and how I lived with them. I am beginning my ninth year as a cripple, and have learned to try to move slowly, with concentration, with precision, with peace. Forgetting plastic bags in the first set of drawers and having to turn the chair around to get them is nothing. The memory of having legs that held me upright at this counter, and the image of simply turning from the counter and stepping to the drawer, are the demons I must keep at bay, or I will rage and grieve because of space, and time, and this wheeled thing that has replaced my legs. So I must try to know the spiritual essence of what I am doing.

On Tuesdays when I make lunches for my girls, I focus on this: The sandwiches are sacraments. Not the miracle of transubstantiation, but certainly parallel with it, moving in the same direction. If I could give my children my body to eat, again and again without losing it, my body like the loaves and fishes going endlessly into mouths and stomachs, I would do it. And each motion is a sacrament, this holding of plastic bags, of knives, of bread, of cutting board, this pushing of the chair, this spreading of mustard on bread, this trimming of liverwurst, or ham. All sacraments, as putting the lunches into a zippered book bag is, and going down my six ramps to my car is. I drive on the highway, to the girls' town, to their school, and this is not simply a transition; it is my love moving by car from a place where my girls are not to a place where they are; even if I do not feel or acknowledge it, this is a sacrament. If I remember it, then I feel it too. Feeling it does not always mean that I am a happy man driving in traffic; it simply means that I know what I am doing in the presence of God.

If I were much wiser, and much more patient, and had much greater concentration, I could sit in silence in my chair, look out my windows at a green tree and the blue sky, and know that breathing is a gift; that a breath is sufficient for the moment; and that breathing air is breathing God.

ON THE LAST DAY OF MY FATHER'S LIFE, HE WAS THIRSTY AND HE asked me to crush some ice and feed it to him. I was a Marine captain, stationed at Whidbey Island, Washington, and I had flown home to Lake Charles, Louisiana, to be with my father before he died, and when he died, and to bury him. I did not know then that the night flight from Seattle was more than a movement in air from my wife and four young children to my dying father, that every moment of it, even as I slept, was a sacrament I gave my father; and they were sacraments he gave me, his siring and his love drawing me to him through the night; and sacraments between my mother and two sisters and me, and all the relatives and friends I was flying home to; and my wife and children and me, for their love was with me on the plane and I loved them and I would return to them after burying my father; and from Time itself, God's mystery we often do not clearly see; there was time now to be with my father. Sacraments came from those who flew the plane and worked aboard it and maintained it and controlled its comings and goings; and from the major who gave me emergency leave, and the gunnery sergeant who did my work while I was gone. I did not know any of this. I thought I was a son flying alone.

My father's cancer had begun in his colon and on the Saturday before the early Sunday morning when he died, it was consuming him, and he was thin and weak on his bed, and he asked for ice. In the kitchen I emptied a tray of ice cubes onto a dish towel and held its four corners and twisted it, then held it on the counter and with a rolling pin pounded the ice till it was crushed. This is how my father crushed ice, and how my sisters and I, when we were children, crushed it and put it in a glass and spooned sugar on it, to eat on a hot summer day. I put my father's ice into a tall glass and brought it with an iced tea spoon to the bedroom and fed him the ice, one small piece at a time, until his mouth and throat were no longer dry.

As a boy I was shy with my father. Perhaps he was shy with me too. When we were alone in a car, we were mostly silent. On some nights, when a championship boxing match was broadcast on the radio, we listened to it in the living room. He took me to wrestling matches because I wanted to go, and he told me they were fake, and I refused to believe it. He took me to minor league baseball games. While we listened to boxing matches and watched wrestling and baseball, we talked about what we were hearing and seeing. He took me fishing and dove-hunting with his friends, before I was old enough to shoot; but I could fish from the bank of a bayou, and he taught me to shoot my air rifle; taught me so well that, years later, my instructors in the Marine Corps simply polished his work. When I was still too young to use a shotgun, he learned to play golf and stopped fishing and hunting, and on Saturdays and Sundays he brought me to the golf course as his caddy. I did not want to caddy, but I had no choice, and I earned a dollar and a quarter; all my adult life I have been grateful that I watched him and listened to him with his friends, and talked with him about his game.

My shyness with him was a burden I did not like carrying, and I could not put down. Then I was twenty-one and a husband and a Marine, and on the morning my pregnant wife and I left home to drive to the Officers' Basic School in Quantico, Virginia, my father and I tightly embraced, then looked at each other's damp eyes. I wanted to say *I love you,* but I could not.

I wanted to say it to him before he died. In the afternoon of his last day, he wanted bourbon and water. A lot of ice, he told me, and a lot of water. I made drinks for my sister and me too, and brought his in a tall glass I did not hold for him. I do not remember whether he lifted it to his mouth, or rested it on his chest and drank from an angled straw. My sister and I sat in chairs at the foot of the bed, my mother talked with relatives and friends in the living room and brought them in to speak with my father, and I told him stories of my year of sea duty on an aircraft carrier, of my work at Whidbey Island.

Once he asked me to light him a cigarette. I went to his bedside table, put one of his cigarettes between my lips, lit his Zippo, then looked beyond the cigarette and flame at my father's eyes: They were watching me. All my life at home before I left for the Marine Corps, I had felt him watching me, a glance during a meal or in the living room or on the lawn, had felt was trying to see my soul, to see if I were strong and honorable, to see if I could go out into the world, and live in it without him. His eyes watching me light his cigarette were tender, and they were saying good-bye.

That night my father's sisters slept in the beds that had been mine and my sister's, and she and I went to the house of a neighbor across the street. We did not sleep. We sat in the kitchen and drank and cried, and I told her that tomorrow I would tell my father I loved him. Before dawn he died, and for years I regretted not saying the words. But I did not understand love then, and the sacraments that make it tactile. I had not lived enough and lost enough to enable me to know the holiness of working with meat and mustard and bread; of moving on wheels or wings or by foot from one place to another; of holding a telephone and speaking into it and listening to a voice; of pounding ice with wood and spooning the shards onto a dry tongue; of lighting a cigarette and placing it between the fingers of a man trying to enjoy tobacco and bourbon and his family as he dies.

Gladly

DAVID JAMES DUNCAN

As a child I was taught by certain pious adults that what is funny or pleasurable, and what is holy, are two separate categories. When I was twelve years old, for instance, I was thrown out of church one weekday evening by a Seventh Day Adventist man veiny with rage, for playing the Ramsey Lewis version of "Hang On Sloopy" on the church's grand piano.

"This is *God's House*!" the man roared in my face.

"That was Ramsey Lewis," I peeped in reply.

"Get out!" he bellowed, seizing me by the scruff of my blazer.

"Okay," I piped, and left.

It was a gorgeous piano, that one in the church: a big black Baldwin grand. The music I'd been playing was the first rhythm-and-blues my scrawny white fingers had ever mastered. The church had been empty. In Buddhism, Emptiness is God. I don't know who Sloopy is in Buddhism, but in the song he's the protagonist. "Hang on, Sloopy!" the song tells him again and again. "Hang on!" To what? Maybe emptiness.

I'd been playing Bach for years, and loved Bach. Hearing Ramsey Lewis, though, it seemed probable that any God in whose image I was made would enjoy him, too. Rhythm and blues was to Bach what Mary Magdalene was to the Blessed Virgin Mary. Ramsey Lewis bent notes the way Yogi Berra bends words. "Hang on Sloopy" was, at the time, the most exciting piece of music I had in me, and it felt great making it fly out into the church's vast emptiness. The other kids loved it, too—till the Adventist God's cocksure sergeant-at-arms came roaring in and filled us all with guilt.

So I never felt the truth of what that man did; never understood why the piano's location in "God's House" forbade my choice of the song; never was able to believe in his God. I still don't—though the man seems to have cloned himself, bought several broadcasting networks and a political party, and set out to turn all of America, Washington D.C., first, into a graven image of himself.

I was reminded of this "Hang on Sloopy" fiasco a few years ago, when I heard about a boy who'd named his teddy bear Gladly.

"Why Gladly?" someone asked him.

"'Cause he's cross-eyed," the boy said.

"What's crossed eyes got to do with the name Gladly?" the questioner wondered.

"We sing it at church," the kid explained. "It's a hymn. Called 'Gladly My Cross I'd Bear.'"

I never learned the name of that kid. I wonder whether he wasn't related to Yogi Berra. At any rate, when I heard about him and his bear, then thought of Jesus and his terribly unfunny cross, then tried to decide whether there was anything blasphemous about the kid's misunderstanding of the hymn title, I thought of Christ's words, *"Whosoever shall not receive the kingdom of God as a little child shall in no wise enter . . ."* And it occurred to me that if Christ did not find "Gladly the Cross-eyed Bear" funny, even in spite of the manner of his death, his words about the kingdom of God would be a lie.

I have bet my literary and spiritual life on the belief that Christ is not a liar. I have staked my life on an intuition that Jesus *does* find the likes of Gladly funny, and that once upon a time he found another kid's R & B piano-playing palatable enough, too.

One more story about one more song.

My oldest brother's favorite Christmas carol was "The Little Drummer Boy." My oldest brother was my best friend when I was a boy. When this brother died at seventeen, he wasn't worth much in the way of property, but I missed him, "sorely" as the Gospels might put it. So I longed to inherit as many as possible of the few things he did own. One of those things was his preference for "The Little Drummer Boy." I began to claim it as my favorite carol, too. Of course my favoritism was based solely on my brother. I'd been partial to a Ramsey Lewis-like version of "Good King Wencaslaus" myself. As time passed, though, "The Little Drummer Boy" began to grow on me. Because just think about its premise:

Here was some kid standing next to the cradle of a newborn baby, banging away on a *drum*. Has any vindictive relative ever given a child in your home a drum? Pah rum pah pum pum is an extremely kind description of the result. Yet, out of reverence and love, the "poor Boy" marched right up to the Christ child's manger and banged the hell out of his drum. The unseemliness of this began to appeal to me deeply: it spoke to the unseemliness of my brother's early death, and Christ's death, too, I suppose. I pictured the infant Jesus' eyes, unable to focus but going wide at the loud banging. I pictured God wincing, wanting to cover His son's ears or stop the banging somehow, but then thinking, "Nope. These are mortals, this is Earth, this is my son among the mortals. Let the boy drum."

True, the carol is just a devout work of fiction. It's not likely that such a scene occurred in Bethlehem. But what about every-where on earth since? If Christ is, as I choose to believe, still alive today, and still listening to anything as multifarious and awkward and half-baked as the prayers and thoughts we offer him and paltry gifts we bring, then the ear-pounding definitely goes on.

My feeling about God is that our imperfect attempts to wor-ship Him are inevitably and almost infinitely silly, inappropriate, and unworthy—my own remark about "God wincing" being a case in point. My sense is that God, in his inconceivable Majesty, is being infinitely insulted, all the time. Yet as I read the world's great wisdom Traditions—Christian, Hebraic, Islamic, Buddhistic and Vedantic alike—I am filled with wonder to find that God, or Emptiness, call Him what you will, *wants* this infinity of insults; that he even *requests* them; that he goes so far as to demand, from the would-be-faithful, every Gladly the Bear, bent-stringed blues note and baby-waking drumbeat we're able to muster, as long as they're mustered with a whole heart.

So every December, the first time I hear "The Little Drummer Boy," especially if it's sung by children, the chills run clear up to my eyes as the sweet truth of the fiction hits home. That it's "a poor boy, too"—same as Christ: the truth of our spiritual poverty gets me every time.

Then the line, *I played my best for him pah rum pah pum pum* . . . What more can one offer, no matter how silly or bad it sounds? And the line, *He smiled at me pah rum pah pum pum* . . .

What more can one aim or hope for then to please the Emptiness, child king, or audience one sets out to honor? I believe—based on the Gospels, and the words of the excommunicated Meister Eckhart, and the non-Christian Simone Weil, and the Beguine saints burned at the stake by Christians; I believe, based on the Bhagavad Gita, Sufi poets, Ramayana, Mahabharata, Buddhist sutras and Tao te Ching; I believe based on intuition, love, my lifelong experience of my own spiritual incompetence, and my departed brother's favorite carol—that all human knowledge and praise of God, in relation to That which it purports to approach or regale, will forever be so battered and bent-stringed and full of half-truths, untruths, drum-whacks, and theological Yogi Berra-isms that we have no choice but to come unto Truth "as little children." This, I'd wager, is exactly why Christ recommends the strategy.

It might be nice to come unto Him as sagacious if hopelessly sexist Pauline patriarchs, or forget-love-convert-thy-neighbor tel-evangelical "Christian soldiers," or perfect-pitched Pavarotti-voiced angels who'd no doubt scare the baby even worse than the drum. But that isn't the drill as the Gospels define it. Our tangled natures, according to Jesus anyway, leave God no choice but to accept every last tangled prayer and scrap of inappropriate praise and bent-noted blues ditty and silence-rending drum-whomp his dopey children can manage to offer.

And I say, thank God, thank the Maker of trout streams, thank emptiness, that we're asked.

I believe Jesus was no liar. Which is not to say that the man who threw me out of the church building was. R & B piano, cross-eyed bears and the drumming of poor boys may *not* belong in such buildings. All I'm saying is that, if they don't, such buildings hold no entry into the kingdom of God.

Six Prayers

MARY GORDON

For Liars

FOR MAKERS OF ELABORATED WORLDS, ADORNED AND PEOPLED BY the creatures and the furniture of their inventions. For those who live as if the way things are were not enough and mean, by their words, to do something about it. For those who would protect the first beloved from the fresh reality of the second. For fabricators of plausible excuses that will save the fragile hostess's *amour-propre*. For ornamenters who cannot endure a history without clear heroes and sharp villains. For speakers of the phrases "it's a fabulous haircut" of "of course you aren't gaining weight." For advertisers presenting a paradise that can be bought or cures passed quick, over the counter, sellers of temporary, unlikely, but not impossible hopes: the Brooklyn Bridge, the golf course in the swamp. Keep them from the terror of the hunted, the ring of hounds barking in the freezing air, "the truth, the truth, why can't you tell the truth for once?" Shelter them in their dream of an earth more various than our own. Preserve them from diseases of the tongue, the mouth, the lips. For Your sake, who have thought of universes not yet made, which rest, like lies, in the Mind of Your Infinite Love.

For Those Whose Work Is Invisible

FOR THOSE WHO PAINT THE UNDERSIDE OF BOATS, MAKERS OF ornamental drains on roofs too high to be seen; for cobblers who labor over inner soles; for seamstresses who stitch the wrong side of linings; for scholars whose research to no obvious discovery; for dentists who polish each gold surface of the fillings of upper molars; for sewer engineers and those who repair water mains; for electricians; for artists who suppress what does injustice to their visions; for surgeons whose sutures are things of beauty. For all those whose work is for Your eyes only, who labor for Your entertainment, or their own, who sleep in peace or do not sleep in peace, knowing that their effects are unknown.

Protect them from downheartedness and from diseases of the eye.

Grant them perseverance, for the sake of Your love, which is humble, invisible and heedless of reward.

For Those Who Devote Themselves to Personal Adornment

FOR OFFICE WORKERS WHO HAVE FALLEN INTO DEBT BECAUSE they spend their salaries on dresses, for women who require regular appointments with podiatrists to compensate for the ravages of years in high heels, for the victims of disastrous plastic surgery, for those who deprive themselves of sugar, for invalids who rise from bed only to dress and make up and then fall back exhausted, for those who weep in front of mirrors, for those with great legs and bad tempers, for mutton dressed as lamb, for those who sweat and strain their muscles out of fidelity to the illusions of a form.

Spare them diseases of the skin and teeth, for in their sacrifice of time and health and friendship they have given hope to strangers whose hearts have been lifted at the sight of a line that finishes itself finely, of colors undreamed of by nature, of constructions which at once affirm and quite deny the body's range.

Bless them because a change of fashion can allow us to believe there could just be, for all of us, a change of heart.

Grant this for the sake of Your love, which has adorned the mountains and created feathers and elaborate tails, O Lord, source of all that exists for delight only, for display only, suggestions, in the joy of their variety, of the ecstasy of light which is eternal, change-less and ever-changing.

For Those Who Have Given Up Everything for Sexual Love

O LORD, FOUND TO DESIRE AND ITS SOURCE, HAVE MERCY ON these Thy servants who have followed the words of their flesh in the innocence of its singleness. Who have acted in accordance with its urging and obeyed it in humility, bowing the knee before its strength, knowing it greater than their own. Who have, in unity with its precepts (believing they were spoken in Your voice), turned their backs on the sweetness of habit, lost the regard of their fellows, endured the world's shame, suffered remorse, the abandonment of those by whom they knew and named and rec-ognized themselves. Who have refused the blandishments of pros-perity, the comforts of home, the pride of faithfulness, the honor of law.

Protect the reckless, for they have lost everything in Your name, their losses have been great.

Keep them from the plagues that they could understand as punishment.

Vouchsafe that in the light proceeding from Your light, they may reap the rewards of their sacrifice and be repaid a hundredfold.

Grant that we who have lacked their courage may be strength-ened by their example to pursue our partial loves with gladness and fullness of heart.

For the Wasteful

O GOD, IN YOUR BENEVOLENCE LOOK WITH KINDNESS UPON those who travel first class in high season, on those who spend whole afternoons in cafes, those who replay songs on jukeboxes, who engage in trivial conversations, who memorize jokes and card tricks, those who tear open their gifts and will not save the wrapping, who hate leftovers and love room service, who do not wait for sales. For all foolish virgins, for those who knowingly give their hearts to worthless charmers, for collectors of snowman paperweights, memorial cups and souvenir pens. For those who take the long way home.

We pray to You, whose love is prodigal, who multiplied the loaves and fishes so that there were baskets upon baskets left, who turned plain water into wine of a quality no one required, who gave Your life when You need only have lifted a finger, protect these, Your servants, from afflictions of the hand, cover their foolish bets and greet them with that mercy whose greatness is unearnable by calculation or by thrift.

For Those Who Misuse or Do Not Use or Cannot Use Their Gifts

FOR CONSERVATORY-TRAINED COMPOSERS OF INCIDENTAL MUSIC, for beauties run to fat, for the patrons of charlatans, for athletes who watch television, for poets who write commercials, for mathematicians turned card-sharks, for Legal Aid lawyers turned corporate counsel, for actors who are waiters, for wives who do not wish to stay at home, for cat-lovers afraid of mess, for paramours who fear transmittable diseases, for those who no longer go to auditions, for blacksmiths and letterpress printers.

Lord who created manna in the desert and who caused to flow the living springs, who made disciples of fisherman and tax collectors, and a king of a shepherd boy, grant these Thy servants the gift of new enthusiasms, protect them from diseases of the spine, so that they may turn and bend to glimpse Your Hand at the fork of roads not taken, at the tunnel's end.

Offer It Up

TONY HILLERMAN

YOU MUST GET ACQUAINTED WITH MAMA, MY HERO. WITHOUT HER understanding I would never have had a chance to wear the combat infantry badge, which we former grunts consider America's highest military decoration, nor would I have become a writer.

Mama's own life had taught her that youth must have its adventures, whatever the risk. (And she'd had adventures herself: homesteading 160 acres in what is now Beaver County, Oklahoma; and serving as an Army nurse in the First World War; and most of all marrying my dad, then a widower with tow teenage daughters—now *that* was brave.) She passed that wisdom along, and also somehow taught me that daydreaming has its values. Her most important lesson was not be afraid of anything. Since God loves us, there is no rational justification for fear. If we do our part by using the good sense He gave us, He's not going to let anything happen that isn't somehow or other for our own good.

Mama could create a tale of magic for her kids while bandaging a skinned knee, canning beets, or turning the hand-cranked clothes wringer beside the washtub. She was our singer of songs, reader of fairy tales, maintainer of the conviction that we children (despite drought, Depression, and the poverty that engulfed our Pottawatomie County) had nothing to worry about except maintaining our purity, being kind to others, saving our souls, and making good grades. With Papa's help, she persuaded us that we were something special. We weren't just white trash. Great things awaited us. Much was expected of us. Bumps, bruises, and winter colds were not to be complained about; whining and self-pity were not allowed.

"Offer it up," Mama would say, hugging us while she said it. When life seemed awful, cruel, and unfair, Mama would remind us that it was just a brief trial we had to endure, a race we had to run, a test we must pass as best we could. We were born, we'd live a little while, and we'd die. Then would come joy, the great reward, the Great Adventure, eternal life. So, children, never, never be afraid.

Papa's instructions were more specific. Our kinds of people never lie, never steal, never cheat. And maybe most important of all, Hillermans never judge others. We're all God's children and we'd leave the judging to God. That meant we couldn't be racist. But he never gave us a specific prohibition. For example, the autumn before he died he called my brother Barney and me in, told us he had been hearing some disturbing reports about the pool hall in Konawa. "I'd be disappointed if you boys went in there," he said, and I didn't go into a pool hall until years after he was dead. Or, when he discovered I had been missing the school bus and making the two-mile walk down to the South Canadian river to wile away the hours daydreaming in the shade, telling me I might be happier staying home and helping with the work. I tried that one day, and never played hooky again.

OUR CHURCH WAS BUILT AT THE SUMMIT OF CHURCH HILL, THE highest hill in our part of Oklahoma. Therefore when I sat in the shade of its trees to think boyhood thoughts I could (by Pottawatomie County standards) see forever. The hilltop was first to enjoy a breeze and the church interior was cool and dim, and breathed with the perfume of Sunday's incense, old wood, candle smoke, and a sense of God's presence. Sometimes the church was locked because of rumors that the Ku Klux Klan was planning arson. But I had become our self-appointed librarian and that gave me not only access but a reason to be wiling away my idle time atop Church Hill.

The library, of which I was both founder and sole patron, occupied a storeroom adjoining the sanctuary. Its books were the odds and ends left behind when the Benedictines moved their school to Shawnee to become St. Gregory's College. Some were in Latin, German, or French and undecipherable for me. I had found them collecting dust in stacks of boxes one Sunday, nosing around after doing my turn as altar boy at Mass. I told the young pastor we had at the time I'd sort them out and make a list for him.

Making the list took many a month since I needed to sample contents before penciling in title, author, subject, and publication date into my Big Chief notebook. I started with Plutarch's *The Lives of Famous and Illustrious Men of Greece and Rome*, a sort of gossipy account of the machinations and misdeeds of the movers and shakers of the Classic Age and pretty racy stuff for a sixth grader. Then followed Prescott's *Conquest of Peru* and *Conquest of Mexico*, Darwin's *Evolution of Species*, Washington Irving's *Conquest of Grenada*, and so forth. I dipped into *The Lives of the Saints* now and then for a change of pace.

Such reading provide an endless source of questions for Father Bernard to answer and answer he did. Darwin's theories, said he, didn't conflict with our biblical Genesis stories because we understood that in these God taught in poetic metaphor. The biblical "days" of creation represented eons of time. Humanity separated us from the other primates when God touched the first of us with self-knowledge of Him and of life, death, good, and evil. The evolution theory was simply a brilliant scientist's attempt to help us understand the dazzling complexity of God's creation—from the amazing strength of a grasshopper's legs to the way our brains translated the signals delivered by our optic nerves. Father Bernard made the Gospels equally simple. Christ tried to teach us that happiness lay in helping others, selfishness was the road to damnation. His bottom line always boiled down to God loves us. He gave us free will, permission to go to hell if we wanted, rules to follow if we preferred both a happy life and heaven, and a conscience to advise us along the way.

God's Love on a Darkling Plain

Barry Lopez

MANY YEARS AGO, CAMPED ON OPEN TUNDRA IN NORTHERN Alaska with a friend and waiting for a bush plane to pick us up, I hiked away across land that stretched on for miles. The rolling and treeless vista that I scanned as I ambled is what biologists call mesic tundra, an ecosystem of cold-adapted sedges, forbs, and other plants living in damp soil during a brief summer, vegetation that rises no more than a few inches from the ground. That same few inches below the surface, the ground is permanently frozen.

Under a solid deck of low gray cloud (a cover that made locating us too dangerous and haphazard a task for the pilot meant to fetch us), the tundra palette was a hundred shades of brown and tan. Tiny pindots of red within it, and of yellow, white, and purple, were too minuscule to register on the retina unless close at hand. The long, simple sketchline of this landscape, the flat light and lack of color, and the absence of any animals in that particular hour—no snow geese skying over my head, no pair of ducks alighting on a melt pond of matte-black water, no distant drift of browsing caribou, no wolf or fox loping through—gave the plain a melancholy look. The dreariness and chill air might have inspired Sibelius's *Swan of Tuonela*.

I've attended to enough landscapes the world over to know the sadness I perceived here was culturally induced, that it was a projection. The land has an intrinsic nature, and in that moment

I was aware of only a sliver of the reality spread out before me. The gloomy prospect, nevertheless, urged the feeling that grows from the contemplation of human messes, the sentimental pessimism about human failure the Germans call *Weltschmerz*. As I pursued a looping hike that day across the shallow ridge-and-swale of damp tundra, a phrase hung before me: *peccata mundi,* the sins of the world.

I don't know what called the words up. The melancholy aspect I'd fixed on in the landscape, of course, triggered the thought. But the phrase gathered strength because it was reinforced by the memory of terrible cruelty I'd witnessed in public streets everywhere: drunken belligerence, abandoned children, mutilated animals, starvation, goon violence, the commonplace evidence of a destructive and apparently ineradicable waywardness in us.

Confronting the viciousness of human life in places like Nairobi or Manaus or Karachi or Sarajevo or The Bronx, one quickly condemns the perpetration; but that day, brooding over it on the tundra, I felt compassion for humanity more deeply. We're as noble as we are base, as intent on serenity as revenge. We injure when we mean no harm, we destroy the things we love, we succumb to prejudice even as we strive for justice.

It's a Church phrase, *peccata mundi,* and strictly speaking a concept of sin is not universal. Wanting to forgive humanity its transgressions, however, I can imagine is a universal impulse. To look deeply into one's self is to discover the capacity to produce horror; it may be our belief that it is morally wrong completely to condemn our own nature that makes us feel compassion and forgiveness toward others, even strangers.

I don't remember what specifically I was reflecting on that day on the tundra, but it could have easily been Buchenwald, or the Turkish slaughter of Armenians three decades earlier, or something as prosaic as the destruction of indigenous culture in the Mato Grosso today, the quotidian work of mining, logging, and construction enterprises and well-intentioned missionaries. But I remember the impasse of this conundrum: I don't know how to forgive the Gestapo and the Schutzstaffel for what they did at Buchenwald. I don't know how one forgives the capitalists who have wreaked cultural and environmental havoc on the Parana River in the country of the Guarani. But I know you must.

To condemn what individual human beings perpetrate but to forgive humanity, to manage this paradox, is to take on adult life. Staring down *peccata mundi* that day on the tundra, my image of God was this effort to love in spite of everything that contradicts that impulse. When I think of the phrase "the love of God," I think of this great and beautiful complexity we hold within us, the pattern of light and emotion we call God, and that the rare, pure ferocity of our love sent anywhere in that direction is worth all the mistakes we endure to practice it.

To walk away from the shelter of the tent that afternoon, to see what lay before me on the seemingly dismal and monotonous tundra, was to seek after God. It may be a conceit to maintain that the landscape speaks to us, that it might sense our plight, but I believe it does. And to express love toward a landscape that influences us, to seek intimacy with it and to become vulnerable to the world in its presence, is but the impulse to love God. It is to hope, once more, for redemption.

Breathless

MELISSA MADENSKI

MY HUSBAND DIED SUDDENLY ON AN EXHALATION. THOUGH THE majority of arrhythmias give their hosts warnings—a rapid heartbeat, a fainting spell, dizziness—there had been no signs. When we found Mark, his face lay against the car window as if he was dozing. He looked peaceful. No hand clutched to his chest, not even the faintest line on his smooth cheeks that would betray surprise or fear or shock. For weeks after his death, I imagined his last breath, became so obsessed by it that every night, at the time of his death, I found myself gulping in air as if my own breath labored its last. Would he have sighed? Would his breath have caught from a recognition of death? Did he call out last words, *I love you, I don't want to go?*

Our son Dylan was only six years old when Mark died. On the race to the hospital Dylan pressed himself so hard into my lap that I had to shift him away to free my face for the sudden shallow breaths that came staccato-like in the silence. We listened to people say Mark would be okay, because you never know. But we did.

The next day Dylan begged to see his father. When someone you love dies, every bit of you, every thought, every breath, is directed by disbelief. You get so good at making up stories about where he might have gone, at seeing her on street corners or late at night in restaurants, that counselors recommend seeing the body—a hand laying outside a sheet, anything that makes you face that you can't bring the person back by fact or fiction.

39

The room in the funeral parlor was quieted by thick carpet. I told Dylan what to expect, but this was the kid who made every curtain, every shadow, every tree limb into an alien being from outer space. Nothing I told him about a dead body seemed to be as scary as something he might imagine. It would be months before he would ask for Mark to come back and then it was with a wistful tone that echoed the futility of the wish. But that day, he only wanted to tell him "stuff." That's what he'd done the morning before and every morning of his life.

Mark was on a cold metal table, covered by a sheet. I explained to Dylan how, once the body is a shell, there's no one inside to operate it. Dylan gently traced his dad's cold eyelids with his finger. With the oily sweat from his tiny palm, he rubbed his father's brow. He wiped the tears from my cheeks.

He stroked his dad's hair. "He's cold," he said. He looked at the ceiling and asked his dad if he was cold.

"Is he there?" I asked him.

"I think so," he said.

For Dylan, unconditioned by years of turning away from death, it seemed to be the most natural thing in the world to stroke and care for the body of the man he'd loved more than any other, to embrace death with both arms, to see how cold and final it is.

Six years earlier, it had been Dylan who struggled for a normal breath. He had been born prematurely, looking like a featherless baby robin, fallen too soon from the nest. You never know. The breadth of his chest had been no bigger than my fist. His grey skin showed the inability of his lungs to do their work.

Without a ventilator to aid his lungs, he would not have survived at all. A rubber mouthpiece had parted his miniature lips. His face would contort and resemble those of the wailing infants beside him, but there was no lusty bawl to ensure his survival. We would not hear him cry for three days. When the ventilator was removed, we heard a thin wail, like wind sliding past spruce and cedar trees close to our forest home.

Plagued from the beginning by apnea—the inability to breathe easily—often he would just stop breathing. His tiny chest would still, then heave with a sudden surge of air into his lungs. A good day was one when Dylan stopped breathing twenty times instead of forty.

Inhale, exhale, inhale, exhale. Stop. The skin around his mouth greyed, the tips of his fingers turned a dusky blue.

The alarm rang.

A caress. A jiggle of a miniature toe. A whispered reminder, "breathe, breathe," accompanied by a physical jolt.

With a shudder, Dylan inhaled. Pink returned to his fingers, lips.

Mark held Dylan and caressed his smallest fingers in the same way Dylan brushed the lifeless hair of his father from his forehead. The touch is gentle, as if the fragility of birth and death can only bear so much pressure.

After two months in intensive care, Dylan's erratic breath stabilized. Five years later it was his sister, our daughter Hallie, in intensive care, her small body swollen from a tear in her trachea so small it couldn't be found to repair. Her voice was lost. My name, when it tried to come out of her lips, was not speech. It was wind rippling past the hole in her trachea. It was a tiny wheezing bellows. It was breath gone wild.

Ruth Sawyer, the fine storyteller, says that ancient peoples believed it was possible to sustain life this way: "the spirit about to depart may be held by one who breathes life out of himself in through the lips of the dying one." Had I known how to breath life back into Mark, to regulate the shuddering breaths of my tiny son, to seal the hole rasping the sweet breath of my daughter, I would have exhaled the soft warm air of life until there was not a wisp of air in my lungs.

NOW OUR BREATHS COME IN LONG SMOOTH RHYTHMS. MY SON blows a mean saxophone in the high school jazz band. My daughter can holler at me from a block away and it seems as if she's in the next room. The departed spirit is held by one who breathes life.

Plato said that when the poet functions properly, he or she is divinely inspired. She or he is "breathed into by God." Mark and I shared the intimacy and rhythm of steady breath between us; the intake of breath at the end of a laugh, a moment of breath's ceasing when we saw each other for the first time after a long day, the unsteady breathing at the end of a hike or a hard conversation. I think, I have come to believe, that his last breath was nothing more than the lightest of exhalations, a prayer, a soft grace.

Holy Places, Holy People

Louis Masson

UNDER THE HIGH VAULTED CEILINGS OF IMITATION GOTHIC churches in Massachusetts and New York, I knelt before the tabernacles that were the holy places of my youth. Before I mastered my letters, I read the lives of holy men and women in stained glass. The schools I attended were always near churches, and the nuns and priests who taught me the names of the stained-glass saints were themselves the holy people of my childhood.

Among the stories and imaginings that nurtured me were saints' lives and picture-book renderings of shrines and holy lands. From the lips of my parents came the stories of St. Francis and the birds, and Blessed Martin, the biracial (though we didn't use that word then) sacristan and apothecary, who spoke to the mice and rats in faraway Peru. Stories of wonder and miracle and sacrifice. And I held these stories, as children do, without reflection or question, and they were, in their way, as real as the church and school down the street.

In childhood the closest I came to the holy places of the stained glass windows was the North American Martyrs' Shrine in Auriesville, New York. There, centuries earlier, Father Isaac Jogues and his fellow Jesuits were tortured and murdered by the Mohawks. The shrine itself is a massive circular structure built of rough-hewn logs to suggest the walls of the Mohawk encampment where the Jesuits were killed. But the grounds around the shrine have close-mown lawns and carefully maintained trails, not unlike those of a public park.

The present nearly obliterates the past at Auriesville. The smoke of the Mohawk fires, the energy of the village that once stood there, even the drama of the faith and blood remains buried; the one exception is the disinterred skeletons of the Mohawks that are displayed in the shrine's museum. Those skulls and bones held my youthful imagination fast. They were not the martyrs' bones, but I saw them in my dreams as the price for sainthood. I measured faith differently thereafter: Isaac Jogues had stepped from the stained-glass window as a dark and haunting presence.

I GREW AND SAW THE WORLD BEYOND THE STREETS OF MY CHURCH. In college I met another haunting Jesuit. I remember the day I saw him first: I sat with other freshmen by the windows of our commons watching the snow swirl in a late winter storm, and across the field that separated the commons and the priests' residence strode a thin spectral figure, erect in the wind, his black cassock and sash swirling, his head obscured by a fur-lined hood. He was gaunt and moved with determination.

"Father Daniel Berrigan," I was told.

As I moved from class and chapel toward my degree and graduation, Berrigan moved from the same classrooms and chapel to civil rights and anti-war movements. His presence forced us to reconsider the boundaries of our faith. As a teacher, poet, priest, and prophet he challenged the authority of the walls that confined our college, country, and church. He made faith dynamic and yoked it to service and political activism. He disobeyed civil law, disconcerted his church superiors, allowed his poetry to drift dangerously close to propaganda, manipulated the national media like a skilled conductor, was hunted down, imprisoned, and wrote epistles from his cell. If he was saintly, he was also quite human. And his life watched from the vantage of a Catholic campus offered a new vision of chapel and classroom. In the debates that he fueled, I could see that college was not only an archive and depository for faith but also a laboratory and creative center. Faith might be recorded and preserved there, and it might also be challenged and redefined. It was a place where shadows as well as light might fall.

As I sit at my typewriter now, thirty years away from my youth, I find that Berrigan has followed me in ways I never imagined and to places as improbable and fantastic as a child's bedtime story. In the glossy pages of more than one of the popular magazines where I take my idle reading, Father Berrigan smiles impishly over a bowl of Ben & Jerry's "smooth no chunks!" ice cream. He is not identified by name, but the small print under his picture informs me that if I "send ten bucks," I will in turn be sent a poster of Berrigan and the seven other social activists in the advertisement, as well as "info" about their activism. The God of my childhood still moves in wondrous and mysterious and perhaps mischievous ways.

NOT ENTIRELY WITHOUT COINCIDENCE I HAVE FOLLOWED Berrigan to a life of teaching at a Catholic university, where I often discover my epiphanies among my students. They come like grace, unexpected but always welcomed. One student was a young Navajo man who was willing to give life to a skeletal lecture about Northwest tribes that I was struggling through: He offered the analogy of his own people.

The young Navajo spoke with a quiet authority that obviously flowed from deep feeling and experience. His voice was older than his face; he spoke from a different place and a different time, toward which his cadences moved us. Briefly he was a shaman communing over a sand-painting with a patient.

As a boy he had slept on the earth and watched over sheep, and time seemed generous. The land where he lived was holy, and so too were the old people, those who still dream in Navajo. His dream was to grow old on the same land. Yet here he was among us, a stranger in a strange land, learning how to deal and live with us so that he might serve his people as a bridge—or perhaps a protective wall. He was an ironic crusader, sent out to protect his holy land by leaving it. He spoke sadly but without self-pity or bitterness. He could even joke about how his residence hall colleagues mistook his ritual pipe-smoking for a more commonplace misdemeanor. They were, of course, partly right, for he was truly "counter-cultural" in his prayers to a different God and hopes for a different life. With great sadness he confessed that he had begun to dream in English. Because of his faith in the spirit of his people and their land, he sacrificed much of his life.

A class bell jarred us back to the world of minutes and books; in Navajo ritual, the sandpainting would be despoiled, the picture erased, and the materials of the picture carried out and discarded. The bell despoiled the picture but could not erase it. Each of us carried away fragments, and I, for one, have held one fragment of his word-painting ever since. His young face, his wise voice, his holy words remain in my mind:

> *smoke*
> *cloud*
> *rain*
> *acceptance*
> *breathing in*

My young Navajo student served the present by revering the past. Both past and present were ennobled by his sacrifice, and I have come to believe that this sort of sacrifice is a powerful way of faith.

IN MY LIFE I HAVE WITNESSED SIMILAR SACRIFICES, SOME CLOSE TO home, some at a great distance. Until her death in 1980, Dorothy Day held a place in my community (and I suspect in other communities and faiths as well) similar to that held by Mother Teresa. Both women are spoken of as modern saints—a designation neither sought. Both lived by faith and both prodded providence in ways that seem beyond the power of most humans.

In the early 1930s Dorothy Day opened houses of hospitality for the destitute in New York City and began to publish *The Catholic Worker*, an epistle more than a newspaper, that became her voice to the world. Over and over she would say that "poverty is my vocation, to live simply and as poorly as I can, and to never cease talking and writing of poverty and destitution. Here and everywhere." By the power of her prayer and the press she addressed and alleviated poverty for over half a century, and she died a deservedly venerated woman.

I never met Dorothy Day, though I was deeply touched by her presence once—not in New York but at Marquette University in Wisconsin. One day on that campus I paused in a Gothic chapel dedicated to St. Joan of Arc. The granite chapel is a fourteenth-century treasure, painstakingly transported and reassembled from the French village of Chasse. It was a small building, solid and intimate. If you bow your head before its altars, the multi-colored light that passes through the century-old mullions bathes you in the past. A few steps from the chapel, in the hermetically sealed seclusion of the university archives, an archivist spread Dorothy Day's letters, journals, and manuscripts on long wooden tables and I bowed my head to read.

Her words touched me much as the little chapel had, because both carried the past boldly into the present. Dorothy Day's faith in providence, her belief that Christ could and should be found in all people—no matter how destitute or wayward—and her work as a social activist all had root in her nearly literal response to the gospel. Her life and her work had medieval patterns. Her houses of hospitality (shelters for the poor, the alcoholic, the abused) and her writings in *The Catholic Worker* sprung from a belief in communal living. Her shelters were a modern equivalent of the monasteries that were hospital, home, and sanctuary in the distant past. She went into the streets with open hands to care for the needy and depended on the goodwill of her neighbors and providence to provide her with the means to extend her work. Her faith was so deep that both answered. And like the granite chapel of St. Joan, which was both anachronistic and beautiful set among the brick and glass halls of Marquette, Dorothy Day's faith remains a beautiful if discordant note in the modern world.

In her life of poverty she allowed herself two indulgences, two simple pleasures: reading and music. Her columns in *The Catholic Worker* represent one kind of testimony, but I found another testimony in her daybooks and journals. They revealed that this extraordinary faith lived in a very ordinary woman. In a 1943 notebook, after a recipe for breadmaking, Dorothy has a list of things "to Learn":

meditate,
sing,
canning,
cheese,
honey extracting,
kill duck,
save feathers.

At the same time that she wrote these things she was attempting to found communal centers that could be self-sufficient in all areas. "Save feathers": The scrap of paper with those words deserves its place in the archives. Too often we see faith as heavenly, but faith is of this earth, nourished by people who wish to learn to sing.

I HAVE FLOWED WITH A GREAT THRONG OF FAITHFUL THROUGH massive *tori* during Oban festivals in Japan. I have washed my hands in the purification troughs and carried from the temples and shrines the odor of incense, the smoke of sandalwood. I've seen the faces of Japan, young and old, rich and poor, at prayer. I've happened upon little temples and shrines in the midst of skyscrapers, places as old as the reassembled chapel of St. Joan. I've heard the gong of a temple bell and listened while Buddhist monks chanted; the sounds were not as foreign as I imagined they would be. I've watched an old and plain-faced Buddhist nun happily give away her only food trusting providence would provide another. And I have been tempted to heresy: to distrust the walls of all religions, even my own, when the stones of practice seem set against the life of faith. I am uncomfortable with anyone who preaches the one true faith. In the name of faith many lives have been taken as well as given.

Once I traveled to an English plain and walked to a university town within medieval walls. By candlelight I sat with dons and students in an ancient hall and enjoyed centuries-old traditions. On that same wide plain I visited a cathedral, also centuries old. As so many others I stood in awe at what faith could build in stone and glass; yet the glass spoke more deeply of faith than I had expected. Huge sections of windows that had once been stained were glazed in clear panes that reminded me of the bleached windows of old warehouses. German bombing during the Second World War had destroyed some of the panels, but stones and bullets, thrown in religious struggles, had shattered others. This cathedral had alternately housed Catholics and Protestants through the years; depending on the era, it could have been as dangerous a place for either faith as a Mohawk village once was for a Jesuit missionary.

I do not like the thought of those blank windows. I prefer to think of the light of faith falling in colors as it did in the churches of my childhood. The blank windows lodge in my memory like glass scars. But there is solace in the notion that time heals all wounds, even those of faith.

There is a sign of this healing on my own campus. Three days a week I teach a class held in the basement of one of the oldest buildings at the University. The floor above my class is composed mostly of students' residence rooms, but there is also a Catholic chapel with stained-glass windows. In the basement, across from my classroom, there is an Islamic prayer room. It is a humble structure, a bit shabby, but faith and learning grow there in tolerance and respect. I believe holiness touches such a place, and touches the people who study and pray there; just as holiness touches the Catholic chapels here, and the church walls and stained-glass windows of my childhood, and the priests and saints and students I have known and loved in my life; a life filled, it turns out, with holy people and holy places.

Spiritual Peaks

GREGORY MCNAMEE

WAS THE EARTH CREATED WITH OR WITHOUT MOUNTAINS? A strange question, perhaps, but one that nonetheless occupied the residents of the Jesuit college of Coimbre, France, for the better part of the year 1592, when the gold-rich mountains of the new-found Americas and of Asia were much on the European mind. Using twists and turns of logic and complex arguments of faith, the seminarians argued pro and con, invoking such contradictory sources as their near-contemporary St. John of the Cross, who urged seekers after the truth to retreat to "solitary places, which tend to lift up the soul to God, like mountains, which furnish no resources for worldly recreations," and the Old Testament prophets, who conversely regarded mountains as frightful places capable of settlement only by Yahweh and assorted demons.

In the end, having determined that the mountains brought humans as close as they could ever come to the heavens, the Jesuits of Coimbre ruled that mountains were evidence of the earth's perfection as the creation of an infallible God. And so the matter rested. Not for a century would it arise again, revived in the fiery words of the Protestant theologian Thomas Burnet (1635–1715), who examined the Coimbre seminarians' argument and countered that the earth was inherently "confused by Nature" and that the mountains were "Ruines and Rubbish on a dirty little planet."

We have since Burnet's time made room in our mental and spiritual worlds for mountains, and Burnet has few modern supporters, I suspect—with the notable exception of the confirmed city dweller Roland Barthes (1915–1980), a sometimes Catholic literary critic who sniffed at the "Helvetico-Protestant morality" of mountain lovers while arguing that qualities like verticality, "so contrary to the bliss of travel," are the hell of ordinary mortals. But we are fortunate to live in a time when the holiness of mountains is almost a given, as the world's religions have always taken it to be. And for good reason: who after all, standing on The Bluff and taking in the vast magnificent sweep of the Central Cascades, could not believe that there, up on 12,300-foot Mount Adams, or the 10,000-plus-foot Three Sisters, or, on an exceptionally clear day, 14,410-foot Mount Rainier, lies a threshold of Heaven?

There on those peaks, the native peoples of this part of the Pacific Northwest say, stands the abode of the spirits, of fierce winds, of the very Creator. There, the Warm Springs storyteller Lucy Miller told the anthropologist Theodora Kroeber, the gods wrestled as Coyote, the Trickster, mightily conspired to keep Mount Adams and Mount Hood from killing each other in a long-ago time. There the earth shook so badly that the First People all disappeared, leaving only the *Klah Klahnee*, the Three Sisters, behind to guide the next people to their new homeland.

On another volcanic mountain half a world away—one that, as University of Portland theologian Will Deming remarks, probably does not exist in time or space but only in metaphor—Saint Paul rose to behold God, pointing the way to a new homeland, too, for his people. And on still another mountain, a 2,510-foot cinder cone called Cruachán Aigle, St. Patrick strode forth to conquer the citadel of the ancient Irish harvest god. He did so, and the mountain, now called Croagh Patrick, is Ireland's holiest peak. As the anthropologist Lawrence Taylor observes in his fine study of Irish Catholic pilgrimage, *Occasions of Faith*, Patrick played on powerful memories when he conquered that height, sacred before as now, driving away the great bird and the monster serpent who guarded its summit; mountains, along with wells and caves, were the loci for the Christianization of Ireland, and today thousands of people retrace Patrick's steps on the first Sunday of August.

They are wild places, those mountains, and terrifying. There is something about mountains that sends humans into states of consciousness—fearful, reverential, even awestruck—that are far from our normal modes of being. Some of the reasons are obvious, even deceptively so. As the Jesuits of Coimbre observed, mountains are for believers the closest points on the planet to the abodes of the gods, connecting the spirit world with our own. Mountains hold obvious dominion over the land, stern royalty gazing down on their lowly subjects. And, of course, mountains are high places, and many people fear heights, although a current pyschiatric index will show you that many more people fear, in descending order, animals, the sight of blood, and being pent up in enclosed spaces.

But from that terror grows a kind of grace. It is no surprise, I think, that Saint Francis's notions of "tendance and comforting" should have arisen in the craggy Appenines, as he walked from Assisi to La Verna, for without such kindness, a contemporary remarked, "in those desolate places man could not live." Grace indeed: the nature of mountains embodies the gift by which God enables us to live holy lives, as Saint Francis knew; they change our being. It is for that reason, as John Muir observed at the beginning of this chewed-up age, that "thousands of tired, nerve-shaken, over-civilized people are beginning to find out that going to the mountains is going home." Muir knew whereof he wrote: not for nothing did he quit the grim industrial lowlands of his native Scotland for the highest peaks of California.

IN MOUNTAINS WERE NOURISHED THE GREAT RELIGIONS OF THE world, nearly all born in the deserts but raised in the high country. The environmental psychologist Bernard Aaronson has noted that "the traditional association of mountain tops with the abode of Deity may be less because they are higher than the areas around them than because they make possible those experiences of expanded depth in which the self can invest itself in the world around it and expand across the valleys," a feeling that resembles nothing so much as extrasensory perception.

That is the feeling experienced, of course, by human beings deprived of oxygen, a sure step toward a coma, and by those who have survived close encounters with death: most mountain climbers, in other words. Alpinist after alpinist reports returning from the mountains filled with an inexplicable sense of inner peace born of that sensory sharpening, filled with something approaching the religious thump on the head that Buddhists call *satori,* like Maurice Herzog's epiphany atop the 26,502-foot summit of Annapurna: "I had a vision of the life of men. Those who are leaving it for ever are never alone. Resting against the mountain, which was watching over me, I discovered horizons I had never seen. There at my feet, on those vast plains, millions of beings were following a destiny they had not chosen. There is a supernatural power in those close to death." And in those, we might say, who venture close to it, as you will read in the pages of Neville Shulman's fine memoir *Zen in the Art of Mountaineering,* an account of terror and redemption on the north face of 15,771-foot Mont Blanc, and in the ninth-century Japanese account of Buddhist monk named Shodo who climbed the volcanic peak Nantaizan to confront his mortality: "If I do not reach the top of this mountain, I will never be able to attain Awakening!" After having said these words he moved across the glistening snow and walked on young shoots glimmering like jewels. When he had ascended halfway, all strength left him. He rested for two days and then climbed to the peak. His joy there was complete, like that of a dream: his dizziness portended the Awakening.

In the mountains the eyes become clearer, it seems, the ears more finely tuned; the customary flavors of food take on new nuances; the calls of birds provide a richer music. The first European known to have climbed a mountain for the sheer pleasure of it, the Italian poet Petrarch (1304–1374), devoted many pages of his journals to describing the odd sensations that overcame him in the highlands, especially on seeing a glacier-lit rainbow atop the small alp Ventoux: "I stood as one stupefied. I looked down and saw that the clouds lay beneath my feet. I felt as if another."

As if another, indeed. The English Catholic mystic Dom John Chapman calls the sense of mountains "unearthly and expanding," echoing the English traveler Freya Stark's notion that the mountains are moving vortexes of energy on a spinning globe—another strange idea, on the face of it, but one that has considerable attraction when you consider that everything on the planet is indeed constantly in motion. I've experienced that "unearthly and expanding" sense on a number of mountaintops: the Zugspitze, in the Bavarian Alps; Mount Evans, one of Colorado's "sixteeners"; on Mount Rainier and, just a few weeks before it blew, on Mount Saint Helens; and, most profoundly, atop Copperas Peak, an otherwise unimposing mountain in southwestern New Mexico that overlooks the rushing headwaters of the Gila River, three streams that pour down from the surrounding highlands and unite two thousand sheer feet below.

In their mountain-studded Alaska homeland, the anthropologist Richard Nelson has observed, Koyukon children learn their place in the order of things from geomorphology itself, having been instructed that they are not to argue over the respective merits of mountains or to compare their sizes. "Your mouth is too small," an offending child will be scolded, meaning that we humans cannot possibly comprehend the vastness of nature. Similarly, the O'od no'ok, or Mountain Pima, of northern Mexico, not far from where I live, liken themselves to ants who crawl along the ragged canyons and massifs of the Sierra Madre, singing an elaborate body of traditional songs that reinforce the notion of our tininess against the high mountains. The Buddha was likely getting at the same idea when he observed, "In the high places of the earth the being is better to look at himself in the face and learn the truth and true proportion of things."

TERROR, VERTIGO, INSIGNIFICANCE: IT IS ODD, PERHAPS, THAT these fundamentally dehumanizing elements should lead to the sublime state that characterizes our best spiritual impulses. The human mind is made up of odd stuff, however, and susceptible to seeing in the land whatever it chooses to. In the mountains, those frightening places, it locates the deities; there is no mountain landscape in the world that is not heavily invested with gods, sometimes from many traditions. Chomolungma, or Everest, is sacred to Hindus, Buddhists, Taoists, and Confucianists alike. Similarly, Mount Cuchama, in San Diego County, is a mountain island sacred to the now-dispersed Luiseño and Diegueño Indians of the California coast, but also to the far-inland Cocopa, Quechan, and Chemehuevi peoples, for whom the distant mountain, rising above the sere desert floor, was a place of pilgrimage.

Saint Theodoros, the Byzantine mystic, held that "a mountain is the image of the soul rising in meditation." The metaphor is apt. Surely Jesus knew the power of landscape when He took up his position on an unnamed mountainside—perhaps it was Tabor, the site of His transfiguration—to give His famous Sermon on the Mount. There He commanded a sweeping view of His followers and the valley below them while enjoying a steep, craggy backdrop that symbolically projected him into heaven, ascending, in the manner of a climber, to attain the ethereal, the clarity, the shudder that the theologian Rudolf Otto finds in the presence of what he calls the "numinous," lying at the base of all religious impulse. It is no accident, I think, that Jesus chose a mountain site to deliver His most powerful address: from on high, there next to God, He spoke of good and evil, of loving one's enemies, of doing's one part in bringing peace to the world; from on high, He taught us how to pray to the Heavenly Father.

Just so, throughout time, in religious traditions the world over, holy people have taken themselves into hermitage in the mountains, there to let their souls rise. Just so, throughout time, we have found peace and spiritual succor in the highlands of the world, where, the Hindu *Puranas* promise, "As the dew is dried up by the morning sun, so are the sins of mankind dried up by the sight of the mountains."

It is no wonder that, the world over, the architecture of the sacred aims to emulate mountains: the ziggurats of Babylon, which bore names like House of the Mountain and Mountain of God; the pyramids of Egypt; the temples of Jerusalem; the stupas of Tibet; the Gothic cathedrals of Europe; even, in this money-worshipping age, the skyscrapers of our urban centers. It's tempting to think that God struck down the Tower of Babel not so much out of anger for its builders' having attempted to unite humans with their maker, but for their hubris in trying to recreate what nature takes millions of years of geological evolution to accomplish: a mountain piercing the heavens.

We cannot undo two million years of our own primate evolution to dissolve the fears and emotions that lie at the center of our beings. Rollercoasters, tall buildings, and a good portion of the films *Cliffhanger* and *The Eiger Sanction* can still produce those beads of sweat that proclaim our fragility, even though we pretend to be masters of our world. In that pretense, overlooking the tininess of which those Koyukon mothers so wisely speak, we are increasingly placing the world's mountains at risk.

Sometimes we do so out of greed. Where two thousand years ago Greek priests climbed the slopes of Olympus and Parnassus to search for signs of lightning, indications that holocausts were propitious and prayers to the gods most likely to be heard, now their descendants build ski lodges; Indian casinos now lie spattered among the once-sacred mountains of Arizona, where I live. And sometimes, with less damage to be sure, we do so out of mere vanity, out of the mere misplaced drive to conquer nature. N. E. Odell, who accompanied the tragic Mallory expedition to Everest in 1924, wondered whether it were right to climb it: "If it was indeed the sacred ground of Chomolungma, Goddess Mother of the Mountain Snows, had we violated it—was I now violating it?" Today, in the race to deprive the planet of all its mysteries, such questions of propriety are laid aside. Not long ago the famed alpinist Reinhold Messner, having secured permission from Chinese authorities glad to offend Tibetan sensibilities, announced his plan to climb Kailas, the holiest of holy mountains to untold millions of people, despite warnings that to do so is to profane it.

Whether we climb them or view them from afar, they continue to pull at us, calling us home, those mountains. Gazing out on the Cascades from the University, watching their peaks pierce the sky, or on the Santa Catalina Mountains closer to my desert home, I count myself blessed to have their sanctuary, their daily reminder of God's gift, and to be able to yield again to tininess, even to terror, and to the ever-expanding universe that lies in the ranges beyond.

Baking Bread with My Daughter

KATHLEEN DEAN MOORE

IN THE CABIN, MY DAUGHTER KNEADED BREAD. THE DOUGH WAS thick, unwieldy, and it took all her strength to turn it. When I looked at her, I hardly recognized this woman-child, her face all planes and no softness. She reached across her body to rub her shoulder, leaving flour on her shirt.

This pain has no logic. It makes no sense. There is nothing to be learned from illness in a person so young. The only fact is pain, and the wooden slab of a daughter's face.

"I don't think of it that way," she said. "You can't know in advance if something's good or bad." She turned to the bread under her hands and pushed against it with her fists. Fists of dough. A rough, heavy dough: sesame seeds, wheat berries, rye seeds. It will make a good thick nutritious bread. "I've seen people who can't tell the difference between what hurts them and what helps them," she said, "and I don't want to be like that." She turned the bread over on itself, and folded over the folding. The expanding dough resisted the turning, pulled away from her fists. The dough had ideas. She pushed it against the side of the bowl. As she kneaded, her face began to relax.

"There is pain that hurts and pain that heals," she said, and I knew she was right. Move even if it hurts, the doctor had told her. With fibromyalgia, this is the way you get well. Healing takes time. Let it hurt, but gently.

Flour and yeast and water. She set the starter on the top shelf of the woodstove and put another log in the firebox. After a time, she added sugar and oil, and more flour, and then all the seeds in the bag. The more she pushed on the dough, folded it over, pressed it with the heels of her hands, the more it rebound. It's hard for a mother, you know, to see a child bear up. I cried in the kitchen, and then I was ashamed. "What's wrong?" she asked, but the pain in me was the pain in her and she divided the dough into two pieces and shaped in into two loaves.

"What I need from you," she said, "is for you to sprinkle corn-meal on the baking pan." So I did. She took a round loaf in two hands and laid it gently on the pan. Then the other.

The loaves are on the shelf under a tea towel. She can't put them in the oven yet, because we've got the stove too hot. It would harden the loaves before they finish rising. So gently now. Not too much heat. I am trying to learn this. Believe me, I am trying. There will be time for more logs in the firebox. We come away and let it rest. Sometimes patience is as good as hope.

TWO EGG WHITES, BEATEN. BRUSH THEM ON THE RISEN LOAVES. Out the kitchen window, there is wind in the birches. Little curls of bark tear away from the trunks and scatter across the patchy snow. The new bark underneath is pure white. Poppy seeds sprinkled on round loaves. Round loaves in the oven, hardening around the edges, still rising in the center. The crust cracks, and steam puffs out the fissures.

Only a few days ago, the birches were noisy with yellow leaves, shuffling in the wind. When we heard leaves blowing across the road, we thought a car was coming; they were that loud. But now the leaves have twisted off the trees and blown onto the lake.

There are fishermen on the bay in their silver boats, leaning over their poles, their hands clasped between their knees; and bear hunters past the portages. We saw them pass today, canoes heavy with gear.

The radio says a cold Arctic air mass is headed into northern Minnesota. There is no color in the sun. Soon we will wake up to a new calm. The lake will be white and shining, with birch leaves frozen in the surface. In heavy coats, my daughter and I will walk on the lake. What will we have about winter? What will we know about stillness that we didn't know before?

Love Is What We Do

CYNTHIA OZICK

WHEN DID THE STUDY OF SACRED TEXTS BEGIN? ONE POSSIBLE answer may be: at the moment when Moses held up the Tablets before the people—the "mixed multitude" that came out of Egypt—the words of moral instruction inscribed on the Tablets. It was at this juncture that ethics fused irrevocably with the idea of monotheism. Yet the showing of the Tablets was rather more in the nature of revelation, manifesto, or declaration, than study.

The true start of sacral learning—conscious, acknowledged, passionately reciprocal—begins with Ezra (Nehemiah 8:1-9): "And Ezra the priest brought the Torah before the congregation both of men and women, so that all could hear with understanding. . . ; and the ears of all the people were attentive unto the book of Torah. And Ezra the scribe stood upon a pulpit of wood . . . and opened the book in the sight of all the people . . . and Ezra blessed the Lord, the great God. And all the people answered Amen . . . And Ezra and his fellow-teachers and the Levites caused the people to understand the Torah . . . So they read the Torah of God distinctly, and gave the sense, and caused them to understand the reading."

And just here, as long ago the fifth century before the common era, is the presentation of a hallowed text accompanied by commentary and interpretation. The people respond with elation "because they had understood."

And what they have understood in this dawn of study and understanding is that the universal Creator is necessarily One, affirming the unity of humankind. (Polytheism lends itself to multiple tribes: the god of my tribe, the god of your tribe, the gods of the other tribes across the river. Polytheism divides; monotheism unites.) The universal Creator, as expressed in Judaism, is transcendent, incorporeal, un-imaged, never incarnate, never immanent, never enfleshed in any form imaginable by human conceptual powers. God's nature is hidden from us, and nowhere is this more mightily addressed than in Job—"Where wast thou when I laid the foundations of the earth? . . . Knowest thou the ordinances of heaven?"—or more clarifyingly than in Deuteromony 29:28— "The secret things belong unto the Lord our God: but those things which are revealed belong unto us and our children forever, that we may do all the words of this Torah."

The divine injunction, then, is not to visualize, imagine, conceive of, or fashion natural or anthropomorphic replications of those "secret things," but rather to occupy ourselves with the tasks revealed to us: to do justly and walk humbly, to care for the window and the orphan, to succor the poor and the oppressed, to love our neighbor as ourselves, and—reaching even further than that— to love the stranger. Compassion is all. (Linguistic note: The Greek root for *womb* gives us "hysterical." The Hebrew root for *womb* is "merciful.")

All this is why I find the phrase "the love of God" intellectually perilous and spiritually demeaning. It leads inexorably to definition, which is to limit, to objectify—and to objectify in subjective terms. It is what Heine meant when he said that if the stones of the hillside could have a god, it would be in the shape of a stone. Who will dare to offer a portrait or any description whatever of the universal Creator? (Even the mystical strains in Judaism, which veer from the mainstream in their approach to Gnosticism—and the Gnostics claim to be God-knowers—speak of God as *Eyn-Sof*, or unimaginable Infinitude.) The love of God, in the sense accessible to human powers, lies not in speculation or meditation or imagining, and least of all in delimiting concretization. It lies in what we do, day by day. And what we do when we do right is not innate: it must be taught, it must be learned. It is a teaching; it has a text, and the text is open to the difficulties and complexities of moral interpretation and instruction. In Judaism the love of God is enacted through right conduct and the study of right conduct; the act of study, concerning itself with the modes of human civilization, is itself holy. The deep study of right conduct is equal to prayer and liturgy; it is the extension and augmentation of prayer.

Our human obligation is not to contemplate God's holiness, or offer our falsifying love to what we cannot understand: that is not spirituality but idolatry. The great teachers and prophets, in every tradition, have always pointed the way not to the unknowable nature of God but to the conquest and rededication of our own nature.

The Meadow

CHET RAYMO

FOR THIRTY-EIGHT YEARS, MY WALK TO WORK EACH MORNING HAS taken me through land in the care of the Natural Resources Trust of Easton, Massachusetts. My path traverses woods, a brook, open fields, an old orchard, and community gardens, but nowhere am I more likely to linger than along the low-lying meadow that floods after any winter melt or major rain. In spring, especially, the water meadow teems with life. Redwing blackbirds take up residence in willow trees along the brook. Canada geese and mallards, in faithful pairs, swim among emerald shoots of new grass. Then comes the magic day in April when the entire surface of the water meadow begins to sing, the choiring of spring peepers, a hallelujah chorus in celebration of new life. Of course, it is not new life at all. Life was there all along, buried in the frozen mud or in hard seed cases on the branches of the trees. Life doesn't come and go; life persists.

Often I take off my shoes, roll up my pants, and wade out into the midst of all this animation, every sense stimulated by the brash exuberance of living things. I know, however, that the real exuberance I cannot sense at all. It occurs at the level of the molecules of life, a ceaseless chemical dynamic: photosynthesis, respiration, fermentation, the zipping and unzipping of DNA, the spinning out of proteins. That fundamental chemical activity is pretty much the same in every creature—frog, goose, blackbird, willow, grass, bacterium; behind the apparent diversity of life is an astonishing sameness. In his autobiographical book *The Double Helix,* James Watson, the co-discoverer of the structure of DNA, tells how he came to think of a helix as the structure for that molecule. "The idea [of the helix] was so simple," he says, "that it had to be right."

I think of Watson's words every time I look at computer-generated images of DNA, proteins, hormones, and the other molecules of life that occur with increasing frequency in the pages of the scientific journals. These molecules are complex—they are made up of thousands, even billions of atoms—and yet they are so simple and so beautiful that we look at them and *we know that they are right.* If I focus on the "atomic" dots of these computer images, I am bewildered by the astonishing complexity of detail, and I wonder that life exists at all. But when I focus on the overall patterns—the geometrical forms and symmetries of the molecules— I am dazzled by an almost inevitable simplicity.

Some images of the molecules of life, as they are displayed on the color computer screen, resemble the gorgeous stained glass windows and soaring architectural members of the Gothic cathedrals. A cross-section of the B DNA double helix, for example, bears likeness to the magnificent rose window at Chartres. And the webbed vaulting of the clathrin protein and the flying buttresses of the sugar-phosphate side chains of the DNA evoke the same sense of architectural *deja vu.* No medieval architect could have raised more fitting structures. The Gothic builders wanted the visible structures of the cathedrals to reflect the invisible realities of the spirit world; the cathedral was conceived as an earthly image of the kingdom of God. Something similar is afoot in the computer representations of the molecules of life. Here, too, there is an attempt by scientists to represent an unseen reality with visible images. And here, too, there is an almost mystical vision of a hidden harmony that has been established throughout the cosmos.

Behind the water meadow's rich diversity of life there is a molecular unity so simple "it had to be right," as beautiful as a cathedral's rose window or flying arch. Abbot Suger of Saint-Denis, one of the greatest of the Gothic builders, hoped that his cathedral would reveal the divine harmony that reconciles all discord, and that it would inspire in those who beheld it a desire to establish that same harmony within the moral order. The molecules of life, revealed by science, achieve the same effect. They inspire a reverence for the invisible harmony—of form and function, of complexity and simplicity—that is the miracle of life. Here in the water meadow it burns like a ceaseless flame.

WE HAVE, IT SEEMS, A FIERCE ATTRACTION FOR DISEMBODIED spirits: auras, angels, poltergeists, immaterial souls, out-of-body experiences. Mostly, I think, we are drawn to these things because we intuit—correctly, it turns out—that there *must* be more to the world than meets the eye. We inherit the spirit world from a time when our ancestors huddled in dark shelters at night and let their imaginations draw up creatures more or less like ourselves though lacking corporeal substance. But why should I care about angels when I hear the croaks of the season's first redwing blackbirds as I step out of the woods onto the plank bridge over the brook? Why should I look for treasure in heaven when year after year the fiddlehead ferns unfurl their silver croziers along the stream's banks? Why should I wish for out-of-body experiences when it is my *body* that connects me through the five open windows of my senses to the sights, sounds, tastes, smells, and tactile sensations of the water meadow? If I want more than meets the eye, I should practice on this: the invisible flame of the DNA.

Even as I stand motionless and attentive at the edge of the water meadow, a flurry of activity is going on in every cell of my body. Tiny protein-based "motors" crawl along the strands of DNA, transcribing the code into single-strand RNA molecules, which in turn provide the templates for building the many proteins that are my body's warp and weft. Other proteins help pack DNA neatly into the nuclei of cells and maintain the tidy chromosome structures. Still other protein-based "motors" are busily at work untying knots that form in DNA as it is unpacked in the nucleus of a cell and copied during cell division. Others are in charge of quality control, checking for accuracy and repairing errors. Working, spinning, ceaselessly weaving, winding, unwinding, patching, repairing—each cell like a bustling factory of a thousand workers. A trillion cells in my body humming with the business of life. And not just in my body. The frogs crying in their hiding; their cells are in a flurry too. The mallards paddlewheeling through the flooded grass. The gelatinous scum of frog eggs at the water's edge. All of it invisibly astir.

Why chase phantasms when the greatest miracle is as close as my next breath? The smallest insect is more worthy of astonishment than a thousand choirs of angels. The buzzing business of a single cell is more infused with eternity than any disembodied soul. Scientists have now provided a complete transcription of the human genome, a listing of the tens of thousands of genes that are the plan of a human life, many of which we share with other creatures. They have found ingenious ways to manipulate the DNA—stretch it, snip it, splice it, watch the protein motors at work, measure their speed. What a thing it is to think of ourselves as manifestations of this invisible molecular machinery, ceaselessly animating the universe with sensation, emotion, intelligence.

To say that it is all chemistry doesn't demean the dignity of life; rather, it suggests that the elemental fabric of the world is charged, as Abbot Suger guessed, with potentialities of a most spectacular sort. We have perhaps an infinite amount yet to learn about the molecular chemistry of life, but what we have already learned stands as one of the grandest and most dignified achievements of human curiosity. Forget all that other stuff—the spooks, the auras, the disembodied souls: *embodied* soul is what really matters. As I stand by the water meadow I try to refocus my attention away from the ducks and geese and trees and frogs, and attend instead to the thing I cannot see but know to be there, the endlessly active, architecturally simple unity of life—the meadow aflame, burning, burning.

Rain

PATTIANN ROGERS

IT RAINED ALL NIGHT LAST NIGHT, A SLOW RAIN. ITS SOUND— thrumming on the roof, multiple in tickings on each separate leaf of the poplar and maple near our bedroom—was very like a caress, gentle, steady. Before sleep, I watched it move in crowds of silver down the glass of the window. And later the rain entered my sleep. It was a cadenced voice delivering an important message in a foreign language I couldn't quite translate.

But once, in my dreaming, I thought the voice was God's.

Rain is such a seemingly simple thing, so ordinary and commonplace. We all must have discovered it very early in our lives, earlier than we can remember. But how shocked we must have been at that first encounter. What an incredible phenomenon— water falling in pieces from the dark kneading and enfolding clouds of the heavens. How extraordinarily strange to move through air filled with water plummeting all around, the sun suddenly dimmed and even shadowed itself. As a friend once told me—watching his infant daughter encountering for the first time the details of our earth—with each new discovery her expression seemed to say, *And this too?!*

The world and everything in it becomes different in aspect in the rain. Rain elucidates and distinguishes with more precision than either sun or wind. It misses nothing, outlining the smallest crevices of iris, honeysuckle, sinking down into the funnels of trumpet vine and crawdad burrow, tracing each furrow in the bark of the oak, dripping off the lashes of green midge and moth, the feather barbs of mallard and coot. It lines the lines of every leaf and spear of the marsh rushes, every pinpoint of the pine, calling attention to each spike of the burr, each gravel of the path. Nothing is overlooked, nothing too small for notice.

Rain even reveals new aspects of the self. Issa, an eighteenth-century Japanese poet, highlights this in one of his haiku:

A sudden shower falls—
and naked I am riding
on a naked horse!

Drenched by the shower, wet as they both are, skin to skin, the man and the horse are altered, the sense of their bodies transformed by the rain.

And rain releases otherwise hidden fragrances—the sudden scent of wet cedar, of water-heavy seeded bluestem in an autumn field, puddle-filled oak leaves piled in ditches, the open earth damp and receptive. A hot cement sidewalk steaming with summer rain smells comforting, a fragrance of human neighborhood to me. The ethnobiologist Gary Nabhan explains the seemingly contradictory title of his book, *The Desert Smells Like Rain*, this way: "Once I asked a Papago youngster what the desert smelled like to him. He answered with little hesitation: 'The desert smells like rain.' The question had triggered a scent—creosote bushes after a storm—their aromatic oils released by the rains. The boy's nose remembered being out in the desert, overtaken: the desert smells like rain."

Rain not only unlocks the fragrances, it also enhances them. So says the poet Kyoshi:

Clearing after showers,
and for a little while the scent
of hawthorn flowers . . .

And rain possesses fragrances solely its own, fresh sky-water in the wind, the cool, clean, sheet-snap fragrance of rain-coming, the trembling and rumbling slow-rising fragrance of rain-passing.

I lived for a time once in an apartment on the twenty-third floor of a high-rise building. To my dismay, I found that I had no way of knowing for certain when it was raining unless I walked to the one window I had and looked down on the street. The rain passed invisibly and silently by my recessed window and me. I heard no sound of raindrops—the roof of the building was seven floors above me, the earth twenty-three floors below. There was little fragrance of rain falling through these city skies; it touched nothing as it flew by. I felt deprived, neglected, as if I'd been left out and ignored, not invited to the party.

Watching rain raining on a lake or pond is mesmerizing. Few can turn quickly from the sight of raindrops striking in chaotic randomness every part of the surface of the water, then immediately losing themselves as they merge into the whole and disappear as separate entities. The resulting radiating rings cross and recross one another, circling, widening, each ring struck again and again by more rain, new rings constantly appearing and overlapping older ones. This vision is the vision we might see if we could see the pattern made by the pealing of many cathedral bells sounding over themselves and over the countryside. Nothing ever really ends or reconciles there. I think we recognize something mythic in that pattern, a basic truth of motion and structure and time, of becoming and dying, something about ourselves, about existence. Thus we are rapt, linked and bound to the watching.

Clean rain falling into the open mouth tastes like the essence of paradise. Rain tastes like life when kissed off the face of someone loved. I pity the stone heart of the moon for its lack of rain.

The last stanza of Robert Louis Stevenson's poem "Singing" suggests another transforming aspect of rain.

The children sing in far Japan.
The children sing in Spain.

The organ with the organ man
Is singing in the rain.

To sing in the rain is a different kind of singing, rather an act
of effrontery, maybe even of defiance, a most exuberant singing.
Witness the famous song and dance of Gene Kelly in the movie
Singing in the Rain. And to laugh with someone else in the rain is
a laughter of freedom and abandon unlike any other. Some of us,
like Samuel Beckett, feel we can even mourn a richer mourning
in the rain:

I would like my love to die
and the rain to be falling on the graveyard
and on me walking the streets
mourning her who thought she loved me.

RAIN IS DRAMA ITSELF AND THE SETTING FOR DRAMA. HARD RAIN
in a thunderstorm is a true terror with its blue-white lightning
rudely, angrily, ripping the vista in half and the explosions of its
thunder shaking the earth with long lingering rolls and growls. The
thunderstorm in Shakespeare's *King Lear* is the perfect mirror for
the inner torment and raging of the king.

In such a storm, all living things in the land seem to draw in,
stop, motionless, attentive and wide-eyed, waiting, every cell alert,
contemplative as Buddhas.

Thunderstorms demand our attention. And afterward, says Shiki,

The thunderstorm goes by;
on one tree evening sunlight—
a cicada cry.

we understand the meaning of peace.

Rain is generally considered a blessing and a beauty, a generos-
ity. He "sendeth his rain on the just and on the unjust," says

Matthew (5:45). When rain comes, it is a gift given indiscriminately—to the tumblebug and the beak of the June beetle, to the hairs of needlegrass and least weasel, the bristles of walrus and peccary, to the mouth of the rattlesnake, the mouth of the deer mouse, the pocket mouse, the thirsty elf owl, the skin of the toad, the spines of the tarbush, alike to murderer, alike to saint.

Says the psalmist,

Praise unto our God who covereth the heaven with clouds, who prepareth rain for the earth, who maketh grass to grow upon the mountains.

Rain is most often a gift nourishing the growing life of the earth. But I'm grateful too for all of its other facets and intricacies, its frights and its serenities, the foreign secrets and whisperings of its motion and coming, the person of its presence. It speaks, it gestures, it indicates, and I sense the universe, I sense myself, anew.

Where God's Grief Appears

PATTIANN ROGERS

IN THE BOBBING OF THE WATERTHRUSH, THE TROTTING
  of the wild boar, in the stiff-legged jogging
  of the nine-banded armadillo, the sideways

darting of the desert cottontail
                      and the drumming
              hindfeet of kangaroo rats, in the flight
  of the bluethroat across the Bering Sea,

the floating of the purple sea snail in its raft

  of mucous bubbles, the leaping of coyote, the springing
          leap of springbok and springtail,

    the green gangly leaping of treefrog, the burrowing

  of the two-gilled blood worm and the scrambling of the flightless
        tiger beetle, present in the scarlet blooming forth

                of claret cup cacti,

      in the creeping of morning glory and the winding
            of kinnickinnick, present
in the gripping of coon oysters to sea whips and to each other,

in wind drifting the seed of cotton grass, carrying
the keys of white ash, the rolling

of tumbleweed, the sailing of white-tailed kite,
the gliding of crystal spider on its glassy strand, found
in the falling of golden persimmons,

the dropping of butternuts, pecans, the rooting

of the fragrant roseroot, in the changing colors of the luring
sargassum fish, the balancing upside

down of the trumpet fish among sea feathers,
in the water-skating of the stilt
spider, the soaring of flying fish, in the climbing,

the tumbling, the swinging, the pirouetting, the vaulting,
in light in living

motion everywhere it appears, as offering,
as evidence, as recompense.

One Clear Chord

MARY LEE SETTLE

I DON'T WANT TO DO THIS. IT IS THE OPENING OF A DOOR KEPT closed for the sake of restful, shallow days.

There are things I know. Not clouds of unknowing, but shards and knives of knowing. The words are tired, *God* and *love*, over-used, twisted, pinned down. To go beyond them is to go into the dark.

God's love for me is easy to accept. Tender and kindly since I was—and that in me still is—a child. But to love God, to admit the love of God?

You have taken away the crutches of my pride, the armor of my righteousness, and sent me into the dark. Must I give up the pleasure of old resentments? Must I reject the moods that define me? Must I look on those who have strengthened me by ill use, and love them for it? I must, or they will be stumbling blocks in the dark.

Must I accept weakness, and learn to admit my love, first, of my silly prideful family, not as intelligent as I, dangerously naive, myopic with prejudice, with a brittle insistence on forming me in their frightened image?

To do that is to let pride in what I have become fall away as the struts fall away from a finished statue, strong enough not to depend on its props to hold it erect.

To see them in my mind's eye when they are alone is to be one with them, not identity, but empathy, the welling of compassion:

my father alone, worried and disappointed, kneeling by his bed to say the Lord's Prayer as he has done all his life, my mother still in the prison of her childhood protections, my brother, ill and bullied.

Forgive that? Forgive them when they laughed at him for carrying a note in his pocket when he was fifteen that said, "If I don't know who I am, here is my name and address." He had had a skull fracture and they laughed at him for being slower than they were. They. Who I must love, the first test of the love of God I seek or find too hard.

Oh, there have been glimpses, like light itself, like the sound that Wilde called "one clear chord to reach the ears of God," that Emily Dickinson called an "imperial thunderbolt that scalps your naked soul," like Mozart taking dictation from the air while he waited for his turn at billiards, his ear so clear, so attuned to that pure sound that he took it for granted, and sometime kicked against the pricks.

Of course there are moments of ecstasy, of promise, and I know them. I am five, and like Martin Luther in the jakes, I sit there, too, and see a huge gold cross in the night sky—a child view needing the comfort of visual metaphor. I am thirty and I stand beside a chair, paused in the act of cleaning, on a morning in London, all concern stripped away, and see without seeing time as a frail, man-measure of an infinite, and realize its human frailty. And standing there for a second, realize that I have been there, still, for a man-made hour or less or more.

Or I lie in bed and wake up in the night, hearing the sea, in a boarding house in Cornwall, held by God as a leaf is held in the hand. Or I kneel in winter behind a house because I have been beaten, not with sticks but with conformity, and know that I am comforted between earth and sky.

These are glimpses of ecstasy, promise, not demand. The demand is that I love You not only in Your cosmic glimpses but in Your presented forms, that there is no choice between love of the world and love of God, that choosing to love this one and not that one, this circumstance and not that one, this judgment called beauty rejecting those presenting grief and weakness and ugliness and greed and timidity and loss.

I have judged by these choices, not as One did, who came into the world to free the world of sin, or righteousness, and of judgment.

In these times, in all times, there is pestilence far away that presents itself as a luxury for me to mourn when I forget to hear the cry from one beside me.

Now the pride, the judgment, fades as the night fades into morning and I know what I am asked to do. I am asked to love this creation, and myself, and my nearest and most judged. The world in all its creating and destroying, is love—not an abstract glimpse of ecstasy, not love of mankind, but of one by one by one as they are blown by circumstance my way, not creation as a massive act too great to contemplate without fear, but the rescue of the weakened gadfly struggling in the ointment.

After the ecstasy of Saint Teresa, in a poem by Richard Wilbur I have kept on my wall to remind me,

Visions were true which quickened her to run
God's barefoot errands in the rocks of Spain
Beneath its beating sun . . .

I know once again that *laborare est orare, scribere est orare, amare est orare* [to work is to pray, to write is to pray, to love is to pray], and I am part of it.

The Waters of Life

BISHOP WILLIAM SKYLSTAD

ONE OF THE GREAT BLESSINGS OF MY LIFE IS TO HAVE GROWN UP on a river, the Methow, which feeds the Columbia. I remember the constant roaring of the river as the waters made their way to the sea—a sound that now calls to my mind St. Francis of Assisi's *Canticle of the Sun*: "Praised be my Lord by our sister the water . . ."

We used the Methow's water not only for drinking but for irrigating our apple orchard and alfalfa field. It was a river rich in fish: In summer and early fall, the salmon swam upstream to their spawning grounds, to exactly the same gravel bar from which they were hatched. We would climb on a high bank or bridge to catch sight of the biggest fish, marveling that four years before they would have headed out to sea as fingerlings. And the river was for swimming and rafting, too, cold as it was; even on the hottest summer days one could remain in the water only for so long before the teeth began to chatter.

Like the change of liturgical seasons, the river, too, went through its cycle of life. The winter transformed the surface of the water into myriad forms of beauty and grace, and then gave way to the swollen, murky river of the spring runoff. That spring river, in 1948, turned destructive, and washed away roads, homes, and bridges. But then, as always, came the summer river, with its crystal-clear waters, and then the lowering river of fall, speaking of lowering snowpacks and receding glaciers, which would be replenished by the winter snows and rains.

I remember looking at the river as a boy and wondering where that water was going, where it would end up. In later years, as I drove through the Columbia Gorge, I would often think that some of the water alongside me in the Columbia River was from the Methow, and some of the fish spawned in my river were no doubt passing by me on their way to the sea. I sensed connectedness, as a boy and as a man, and I remain, today, filled with awe and appreciation of this wonderful gift and treasure in our midst, the flowing waters of life.

THE IMAGE OF FLOWING WATER IS POWERFUL IN OUR JUDEO-Christian tradition. From the Prophet Ezekiel we hear, "Wherever the river flows, every sort of living creature that can multiply shall live, and there shall be abundant fish . . . along both banks of the river, fruit trees of every kind shall grow, their leaves shall not fade nor their fruit fail. Every month they shall bear fresh fruit, for they shall be watered by the flow from the sanctuary. Their fruit shall serve for food and their leaves for medicine." Isaiah tells us, "The Lord will . . . satisfy your needs in parched places, and you shall be watered like a garden, like a spring of water, whose waters never fail." Jesus tells the Samaritan woman at the well, in John's gospel, of water flowing from himself: "The water that I will give you will become . . . a spring of water gushing up to eternal life."

There is something energizing and transforming about this imagery of flowing water. Jesus is baptized in the River Jordan as flowing waters are poured over His body, and similarly the waters of baptism flow over us that we might have new life. Many churches now have baptismal pools with water flowing in them so that the sight and sound of flowing, gurgling water reminds us of the power and majesty of God's grace to us. This belief is beautifully expressed in a fifth-century baptism inscription from St. John Lattern: "The stream that flows below sprang from the wounded Christ to wash the whole world clean and give it life. Children of the water think no more of earth; heaven will give you joy; in heaven hope. Think not your sins too many or too great; birth in this stream is birth to holiness." And we sign ourselves with water, too: "With this elemental element," wrote Roman Guardini, "with this transparent, frictionless, fecund fluid, this symbol and means of supernatural life of grace, we make on ourselves the sign of the cross."

Like the waters, which fall upon our land and make the river, so too will the life-giving waters of Jesus' life give us life and remind us of our connectedness to Him. Single drops of water coming together together, forming a river, remind us of the opportunity we have to live our unity with the Lord Jesus and with one another. The Columbia River can remind us of who we are in relationship to God, of the reverence we need to have for His gift, and of the responsibility we have in using this life-giving treasure.

YET THERE ARE DISTURBING SIGNALS COMING FROM THE MAJOR river of western North America—the 1,245-mile-long Columbia, which, with its tributaries, drains a vast basin of some 260,000 square miles.

Salmon runs have been depleted. Increased pollution is evident. Environmental damage has occurred which will take generations if not millennia to repair and to heal.

The Church, in recent years, has taken very seriously the responsibility for the land on which we live. Pope John Paul II in 1990 stressed our responsibility for the environment. The U.S. Catholic bishops, in the 1991 pastoral letter "Renewing the Earth," spoke about the religious and moral dimensions of the environment in which we live. They mentioned seven themes which are integral to our responsibility for the land: A God-centered and sacramental view of the universe, which grounds human accountability for the fate of each; a consistent respect for human life which extends to respect for all creation; a world view affirming the ethical significance of global interdependence and the common good; an ethics of solidarity promoting cooperation and a "structure of sharing" in the world community; an understanding of the universal purpose of created things, which requires equitable use of the earth's resources; an option for the poor, which gives passion to the quest for an equitable and sustainable world; and a conception of authentic development, which offers a direction for progress that respects human dignity and the limits of material growth.

As a church, we have the opportunity to be a distinctive and constructive voice in appreciating the beauty and complexity of the Columbia River. In the glorious tradition of our saints Benedict, Hildegard, and Francis of Assisi, all of whom had a deep respect and reverence for creation, our work as a community should be to promote justice in our land and reverence for God's creation. Thus we can contribute to the holiness of our times.

THIS IS THE POINT OF THE COLUMBIA RIVER PASTORAL LETTER Project, in which all the dioceses in the Columbia River drainage participated: the Archdioceses of Portland and Seattle; the Dioceses of Baker, Boise, Helena, Spokane, Yakima; and the Diocese of Nelson in Canada. The goal of the project was to apply Catholic social teaching on environmental and economic justice to the complex economic, environmental, and social realities surrounding the Columbia River. We had five goals: to invite all people in the Northwest to reflect deeply on our common spirituality as we explore how this magnificent river connects us; to sensitize everyone to the key ethical dimensions of stewardship of the river; to focus concern on the women and men directly affected by the economic and ecological problems of the river basin; to stimulate the Catholic church in this region to common action that will help sustain and renew the river, and deepen our commitment to the common good. As a Church, we support the common good, and promote a vision of a just and sustainable way for the people of the region to relate to the river and its watershed.

In closing, I would like to share three quotes—two from Pope John Paul II, the third from the Book of Revelation.

"Today the ecological crisis has assumed such proportions as to be the responsibility of everyone . . . its various aspects demonstrate the need for concerted efforts aimed at establishing the duties and obligations that belong to individuals, peoples, States, and the international community," wrote the Holy Father in his 1990 World Day of Peace message. And in his encyclical *Centesimus Annus*, he insists that the State has a task of providing "for the defense and preservation of common good such as the natural and human environments, which cannot be safe-guarded simply by market forces."

From the Book of Revelation we hear, "The angel then showed me the river of life-giving water, clear as crystal which issued from the throne of God and of the Lamb and flowed down the middle of the streets. On either side of the river grew trees of life . . . nothing deserves a curse shall be found there. The throne of God and of the Lamb shall be there, and his servants shall serve him faithfully."

Our river of life-giving water is the mighty Columbia, an extraordinary treasure. May we be faithful servants and stewards.

Spirit-Homesteading the Oregon Country

KIM STAFFORD

WHAT IS IT LIKE TO INHABIT THE OREGON COUNTRY? WHAT happens when you belong to this frayed patch of ground that reaches up along the Columbia drainage, fingers east along the Snake, and ravels out in the Nevada desert of Paradise Valley and the California Siskiyous?

It is like the flavor of cactus leather, fattened by water and stretched by sun. It is like the vertigo of Terrebonne rattlers, caught up dry in a hayload on the east side and broken out wet with the bales in Junction City on the west; they slide off into a swale to confound the biologists and try to shake their rattles dry. It is like the crimson hues and freckles on a trout's belly as it flashes out from a logjam on the lower Metolius. It is like that character my parents heard about when they arrived here in the forties—the woman with the tarpaper hat who hitched everywhere.

"Watch out for that woman with the tarpaper hat," they said.

Rain defines part of this woman, and desert ways, and pluck. I watch for her when I drive. She wears many disguises. (I think I saw her brother riding a bicycle east out of Athena on a hot August afternoon, with a sign on his back: "Doug's Clown Show.") A strange quality in her territory is the abrupt proximity of land-scapes with totally different characters. On the coast, gazing at water's hilarity as it plunges off a bluff into that cove north of Cape Falcon, you could be in Maine, treading the headlands of

Cranberry Island where the waves dash. Yet an hour east from Cape Falcon, floating the Willamette by canoe, you could guess Iowa surrounded you, with the Marion County corn rows and the flat land bragging a midwest bounty. And farther east, camped in a rugged niche on the flank of Mount Jefferson—say, at the place called Jefferson Lake, where bears squall and you lie snug—you could orient yourself for the Rockies of Montana. And farther, beyond the hump of the Cascade range, claim Wyoming. Rain gets shy, and geology naked, in the Fort Rock Valley of Oregon, just as it does west of Shoshoni. You get out on top of Oregon's Steens Mountain, staring down into that hurt white flat of the Alvord Desert, you might as well claim the state of eternity.

All this in one day's drive across the continent of Oregon.

Maybe this sense of being many places in one place begins to account for the sometimes snobbish provincialism of Oregon culture. Visit, but don't stay, said former governor Tom McCall. Anyone who would understand Oregon, said Wayne Morse, must first understand the complete provincialism of Portland. The only way we get a job opening, said a boss to a job applicant in Portland, is death or retirement. Nobody leaves.

Well, that's a sweet lie we love to believe. And there are reasons to believe it. Everyone should believe that about the place they choose to call home.

There are things the visitors don't know, but we know. By local knowledge you can find a dry place at Cape Falcon—hollow cedar, or the heart of a salal thicket massed high over a hollow. You and the hermit thrush. And by local knowledge you know to slide into the hot spring pool that glints on the prehistoric vacancy of the Alvord. People climb naked into the pool and come forth changed.

And I say: Don't pull me from the rain's sweet rush. Don't exile me from sage. I want all of it. I long to walk the fenceline often: two-lane asphalt stitching in and out of fog along the coast, two-track dirt road up past Sky Ranch toward the Ochocos, intuitive deer path along the lip of Hart Mountain. This variety in the landscape has made a home for many Oregon cultures, and the brash internal motley of each local soul.

What holds it all together? A roadmap? History? The individual life? Surveyors use the term "The True Point of Beginning," the place from which all measurements reach. In the early days, this might have been a great old tree, a hunched stone dressed in moss, the mouth of a particular stream foaming with salmon at the freshet. Every legal plot has its own true point of beginning, and every life. Every citizen of this territory has that hub. Where did it start for you?

Was it the time you first heard about the Hoedads, that working tribe of tree-planters roving the coast range with their tools and music? Was it that hitchhiker you picked up who tried to talk you into driving her to the Rainbow Family Gathering? Was it that moment you realized the blue haze of an old pasture was camas in bloom, just like the old days before America arrived? The killing of this place is fresh, and didn't take. The old life of the territory brims like springwater, eager, irrepressible. Wherever I am, I find the true point of beginning again. I fight through blackberry vines where the yard of my Portland rental house falls away into the canyon, through poison oak where the old firs comb the wind, and there I take up the rusted tangle of a kerosene lamp, the thick glass base of a candle holder tossed away in the early time. Oregon history feels like a one-year crop of wheat on a camas prairie—the haze of blue, the shouts of Clackamas just there at the periphery of my vision, my hearing. Living here, I feel that delicious prickle of hope just before a sneeze, just before waking up. The days and colors and seasons of Oregon keep me.

A Georgia grandmother told a friend of mine, "Honey, it don't so much matter where you get born, or where you grow up, but where you catch sense—where the world first gets ahold of you and shakes you awake."

IF MY SPIRIT HOMESTEAD HAS A TRUE POINT OF BEGINNING, IT might be late fall 1949, when the great cherry tree outside the window of my first Portland home tapped the eaves with rain. I don't remember, but my mother says I would gaze and gaze up into the tree, the soft square of the window light falling over me in that little house at the canyon's rim. But where did I catch sense? It keeps happening. You get some and need more.

Or maybe that true point was Tualatin, one morning at the age of three, when I announced to the family, "I'm going to go jump in the daylight now."

"And where is that?" my mother said.

"That way," I said, gesturing toward the east.

"Better take your jacket," my father said. And I set out toddling down the street. That morning, everywhere I could see or imagine was part of home.

Catching sense, setting out, finding the true point of beginning, I survey the territory. I take my staff and follow a river or a road. Thoreau unfurled his steel surveyor's chain into the depths of Walden Pond, mapped it systematically. I unfurl my chain, my tether braided of scent and touch and voice and lightning, out across the landscape to sense these places where they inhabit me.

OUT IN BURNS ONE TIME A WOMAN TOLD ME ABOUT THE PLACE they call Whorehouse Meadows.

"Sounds odd, I know," she said, "but it's part of the beauty. You see, the girls used to take a wagon out there and meet the sheepherders in the spring. It's a lovely place, especially after a hard winter, after being alone. It's a man and woman place. Aren't there enough monuments for battles and deaths and politics—you know, official things? How about meeting, love between strangers and friends? The U.S. Forest Service wants to rename that place 'Naughty Girl Meadows,' get their maps all changed. But that's not right. My husband proposed to me at Whorehouse Meadows, and I don't think they ought to ever mess with that at all." She knew a moment when her life blossomed, and a place that made a story, and that story held it all together. Of single places, the whole coverlet gets made. The Oregon Country contains cultural enclaves quilted into the folds and hollows of the territory. Geology's fist shaped those hollows, rain sculpture, wind work, and the people flowed in, and died to give birth, and stayed. Besides all the occupational cultures schooled by this territory—the loggers who can split a wood match blindfolded, the fishing family crossing the Columbia Bar a thousandth time—a particular ethnic mosaic enriches Oregon. Different cultures among us find their own points of new beginning.

I think of the Russian Old Believers near Woodburn, fleeing their homeland, trying South America, then landing here. It hurt me when our territory struck them as too modern, and some of their number retreated to Alaska for deeper solitude. Maybe we can mature this place by making it quiet enough, and invite them back.

I think of African-Americans, surviving the cruelties of early prejudice at the state's inception, and of Hispanic cultures sweeping through eastern Oregon cattle ranges in the last century, and through the state's agricultural valleys now. I'm haunted by the Nisei apple orchard near Hood River, bought for a dollar when the war broke out. I think of the Hmong, Mien, Vietnamese, Afghani, Ethiopian, and other peoples more recently arrived, how much they give, and give up, to make a home here. I see a necessary part of American history stitched into the Hmong *pandau*, the pictoral "flower cloth" that is both homesick and at home as it shows the mountain village quilted neatly on my wall. What some call "the boat people" from Asia bring to us what the Mayflower brought: a new way of being in this old place.

I think of the Siletz peoples, the Warm Springs bands, the Umatilla, Paiute, Klamath, and all the other original ones still inhabiting, still owned by this place. Where the Chinook people once roved, I think of the Finns working their boats down the tideland channels of the lower Columbia before dawn, startling herons and seeking the silver salmon.

I WAS DOWN AT NASELLE ONE TIME (NORTH ACROSS THE COLUMBIA shoals from Astoria, but well within the generous net of the Oregon Country), where the mayor addressed a crowd in Finnish, told them a story in the old language, and three hundred people laughed till they cried. Then he translated a shorter version of his story for the few paltry visitors like me who didn't know the language:

"I was talking to my neighbor the other day, when he was over helping me put in the new sauna. "How come you're so talented?" I said. "How come you're a fisherman, a logger, carpenter, mechanic, you even weave a little? How come you know how to do it all?"

"'Well,'" he says, "'I'm Finnish. And, you know, a Finn does what he wants to do. Most people just do what they know how to do.'"

And everyone laughed again, in English. And then over at the edge of things, Oiva was telling stories, stories from way back somewhere, Finn stories for this country, and his words tossed out a kind of silk lasso that brought the dead to life. I fell in love with the girl inhabiting his story. Many years gone, she was right there, at his lips, a native citizen of this moment.

The Finns made their Naselle River part of the old country. Here were fish and logs and lefse. And the sweetest thing was a listener, Sue, getting the stories rooted into the spiral of the tape recorder so Finland in the Oregon Country could live long enough to be native, and own it, and be owned by it. Every enclave needs this witness, this gatherer of the voices. Every time I think I know what it is like to inhabit the Oregon country, my neighbors teach me new ways.

One time in Portland it was the Hmong singer Boua who rooted me to this place and all people. We met outside for class, under the apple tree at Lewis and Clark College, and Boua spoke musical, mysterious words about the working life back home, and the interpreter told us little stories from his long talk. "After working in the fields," I said at one point, "would there be music in the evening, up there in your mountains?" The interpreter talked a long time, and then Boua sent a few words back.

"No time for music," the interpreter said, "no strength. Work too hard. But sometimes, in the fields, one could play the leaf."

"Play the leaf?" I said.

"Play the leaf."

"Could you play the leaf for us?" I said. The interpreter spoke to Boua, and Boua sat still for a time, then looked overhead into the apple tree. He is a small man, old and strong. He stood to pull down a bough, and to study it leaf by leaf clear out to the tip. He took one leaf from them all, spread it over his thumb. He rolled it into his mouth, bleated a few times, then sent a flute strand of song into the branches overhead, a song that wavered and dipped like a tired bird's flight, folding the sweet and the bitter into one. A breeze, or something, made the whole tree shiver, made me shiver. I wanted to play the leaf—vine maple, salal, mountain mahogany. I wanted to learn from a new citizen how to inhabit this place in the oldest ways.

I remember one time my brother and I were almost out of gas down in that ghost town of Blitzen, south of Frenchglen. It was dusk, and we saw a light off to the northwest, just at the horizon.

"Let's go straight to that light," my brother said, "through the sage." We drove a long time, dodging brush while the jackrabbits danced in our headlight beams, dodging the car. When the car gave out, that light was right where it started, twinkling at the horizon under stars—a part of the clear air and flat land and eternity. In the morning, a hunter appeared.

"Sure, I've got gas. How much you need?" A neighbor in a distant place.

My father said once that everywhere you look the land held you up. I look, and it seems to go on forever. For a time you will accompany it. This is the place where I was born and my brother died. Maybe I have already survived into the family of the place, and the place owns me.

This territory has a claim on terrible wrongs. A crime is a possession: it possesses me. And it possesses something about the future, something that could turn history as we make it. Desolation bears the seed of hope.

I was driving south toward the Wallowas along Oregon Highway 3 with Phil, my Nez Perce friend. We stopped at the Joseph Canyon overlook, that place where the air goes blue with distance, east, toward Idaho's Seven Devils. I let my mind go. The sun moved. Then we were driving again.

"My family," Phil said, "was not actually of the Joseph band, but was from higher in the mountains. We joined the Joseph band for the fighting, but we were from higher, the lakes." The straight road rolled south through the pines. The land was asking something. "And what do you feel," I said, "coming into this country that was taken from your people?"

"Taken?" he said. "It is here. I am here." Pine sweetened the wind. The car seemed a species of wind, conveying us.

"Yes," he said, "I am here at this place stolen from my people. Some cannot bear to come back to visit, even for a day. It hurts too much. I feel that sometimes. I also feel I am here. I see the places in the stories my elders told me. When they built the new Longhouse at Nespelem, up by Coulee Dam where my people live now, far from this place, we came here to put earth into our moccasins, into our cornhusk bags, our pockets—everything. We took that earth to stamp into the ground at Nespelem, so we could stand on our land when we dance there. The dancing is on the earth where we belong. Someday, maybe it can be made right."

We drove in silence. A hawk circled. If its shadow touched our car, we would feel that point of balance. We would feel that surge where every wrong thing you have done and every right thing together bring you to this exact place and healing. Wind swung the hawk east, over the canyon.

"There is a place at the north end of Wallowa Lake," Phil said, "where old Joseph's bones are buried. I would like to see the summer Longhouse made of many tipis there. Every family brings a set of poles, and we put them all together to make the summer Longhouse. There is a stretch of open ground there, where the river goes, over the hill from the road. We could teach our children the old ways they need. They need to know they belong to this place.

"Joseph said, 'I ask for a place to throw my blanket on the earth. At my home, that is all I ask, a place to throw my blanket on the earth.'"

The hawk had circled beyond us, beckoning. We drove toward the center, where the mountains had stepped back a little to leave a place for the people to gather.

Religion vs. the Media

MARGARET STEINFELS

WHAT EXACTLY IS THE PROBLEM BETWEEN RELIGION AND THE MEDIA? I can think of a pile of problems.

The media's coverage of religion can be absent or banal—trivia of the "appointments and picnics" kind.

It can be obsessive about the sexual crimes of clergy and preachers—Father James Porter, Jim Bakker, Jimmy Swaggart. An erring clergy is endlessly fascinating, as Nathaniel Hawthorne and his *Scarlet Letter* proved long ago.

It can be biased, unfair, and misrepresentative—biased, for example, in favor of America's dominant tradition, Christianity, to the exclusion of some of its classics, like snake-handling.

It can be prejudicial; how many times have we read the word "Muslim" followed by the word "fanatics"?

It can be ignorant; as Michelle Bearden of *The Tampa Tribune* says, most house reporters don't "know a bishop from a Buddhist," and media critic David Shaw has said that beat reporters "are lazy, unwilling to do their basic homework, and display an appalling ignorance of the traditions and influences of religion."

And then there is economics. Some observers say religion doesn't get covered because religion doesn't advertise.

And because conflict and controversy make news (in fact so often *are* the news), religion is at a disadvantage. Good news is not news; when was the last time you read a story about a record soy bean harvest?

So what's being done about these problems?

First, it should be said that for several decades there has been religion coverage of a professional standard in some national news media: *Time*, *Newsweek*, *The New York Times*, *The Washington Post*, and *The Los Angeles Times*, for example, have religion reporters who by training or longevity could be called specialists.

Second, beginning in the 1960s, religion ceased to be a sacred cow and has been "normalized" for the media—that is, subject to the same analysis as politics, blood sports, and Hollywood scandals. Xavier Rynne's reports to *The New Yorker* (collected as the book *Letters from Vatican City*) during the Second Vatican Council opened the door for candid analysis, and the efforts of neoconservatives in the late 1970s to focus attention on what they considered the liberal leanings of mainline Protestant churches suggested that political coverage could be part of religion coverage.

Third, the media has recently begun to give more serious scrutiny to the breadth and depth of its religion coverage—sparked in part by widespread unease over the 1992 coverage of the Branch Davidians in Waco and CNN's 1993 airing of unverified sexual misconduct charges (later found to be untrue) against Cardinal Joseph Bernadin of Chicago.

So things *are* being done, attitudes *are* changing. The Religion Newswriters Association has 265 members, twice as many as fifteen years ago. There is an increase in "religion pages" and sections in newspapers—for example, in the Atlanta, Dallas, Nashville, Phoenix, and San Antonio papers. ABC has a new full-time religion reporter, Peggy Wehmeyer; WNET TV in New York is starting up a weekly religion and ethics news show; the Newhouse chain is making a go of Religion News Service.

But when special reporters are hired, when major obstacles to good coverage are removed, will there still be problems? You bet.

First, good coverage doesn't mean that religions will consider it good. As Mark Silk of *The Atlanta Constitution* writes, "Good religion coverage should make religious leaders no happier than good political coverage makes politicians." He's right.

Second, what is religion news? Is institutional and organized religion really news? Are the annual stories about the Jesus Seminar and the way that its members vote on the "real words" of Jesus with red, pink, gray, and black beads religion stories, anti-religion stories, or horse-race stories? Is a story about Ralph Reed a religion story or a political story?

Third, many religions are exotic and hard to report on. Catholicism, for example. Though deeply rooted in American life, Catholicism is not an American religion. It's not Protestant, congregational, democratic, or small. It makes doctrinal claims that challenge scientific rationalism and reductionism; it makes ethical claims that challenge prevailing American standards of individualism and consumerism. Its very idea of celibacy and sexual restraint make it a genuinely exotic religion in contemporary America.

Fourth and finally, the problem of religion and the media is a philosophical problem. Religion claims that there are truths beyond an individual's experience or opinions; the media often treats religion as a matter of opinion.

Good religion coverage requires not only factual knowledge but a sophisticated intellectual understanding of the unique function that religious teachings and spirituality play in human life. Religious groups need to help journalists achieve that understanding. This might be more doable if they could successfully communicate with their own members by candidly discussing their own questions and anxieties as well as their achievements, anniversaries, and picnics.

If most religious people find their religion news in the secular media, it is often because their own community is not helping them deal with the inevitable dissonances that challenge a religious believer in American culture. This is an intellectual and political task for religious groups, which (rightly) don't see themselves as think tanks or political parties. But if there is to be a place for religious ideas in the modern world, religions must *engage* that world. The media is the most challenging place to do that, and probably the most critically important.

Grace

SALLIE TISDALE

IT ISN'T EASY GETTING EVERYONE TO SIT DOWN TO SAY A BRIEF verse before dinner begins, and it may never be. The small forms are the easiest to lose. We often come to the table in chaos, pulling at each other with little needs the way families do. But now and then the children begin the verse on their own, palms together, eyes cast sideways at each other in shy enjoyment of their own efforts. In those moments I remember why I insist we practice these rituals. It is in those moments that my children and I realize the long, strong bonds of the past, and make another knot in the future.

I'm one of those hard-headed types, an odd mix of pride and insecurity, and my years-long search for the comfort of religion brought me face-to-face with myself. It was hard—very hard—for me to admit that what I longed for wasn't the control and strength I thought I wanted. It was surrender—the long relaxation like letting go of a held breath that comes with giving up control, and bowing your head instead.

I have learned a lot about my own struggle through my children—and through my struggles *with* my children. Finding the comfort of religion, I naturally wanted them to find it, too, forgetting that surrender is the natural province of children. They have no control. Children understand without words that to participate wholeheartedly in a religion requires the willingness not only to give up your lifestyle, but to give up your life. They understand this because, as children, their experience is one of wholehearted participation. Religion risks for its adherents mockery and prejudice, and offers great rewards—and the risks and rewards are not unlike the risks and rewards of childhood itself.

To children, the ethereal and the real are one. The whole of the world and life is magic. They have no fear of the invisible, no shame in wonder, an innate understanding of unity. Children presuppose forces greater than their own. How else to explain how the light comes on when you turn the switch? It is no surprise to children that what we see and hear and feel is only a fraction of what is. They take as obvious that much is unseen. Religion, in providing a vocabulary and a culture in which to embrace these beliefs, is a liberation. By allowing both children and adults the *natural* breadth of imagination, it broadens our image of each other.

Hard as it is at times, my husband and I are letting our children come to religion at their own pace. It is at times difficult not to push, not to chide. They see it in their own way. I keep seeking ways to make religion present not only in their recitations but in their daily chores, in schoolwork, in helping me cook.

Our lives tend to fill with the tasks of daily life, and it's so easy to delay attention to a great purpose. It is even harder as parents, sometimes overwhelmed with the day's mundane demands. But to find the "sublime in the mundane" is part of a long religious tradition. When I am changing yet another diaper, counting to ten with clenched fists one more time, hollering down the block for a wandering child once again, I am engaging in the small forms. My task is to remember this, because my greatest task as a parent is the fashioning of my child's place in the world.

We gaze at the future through the window of our children; how we shape them shapes the future. And they *will* be shaped, by the world if not by us. Each small face harbors the same question, unanswered by self-help books and talk shows. It is the essential question of religion: Who am I and why am I here?

Our libraries are over-full with advice books for parents, with theories of behavior, training, effectiveness. Very few of these books mention religion or spirituality, even in passing, and in a way this puzzles me. It is as though moral training and the lessons of civilized behavior could take place in a void, unhampered by such concerns. Quite the opposite is true. No exploration of morality can evade questions of faith and the possibility of something greater than ourselves. The leading of a moral life doesn't require religion, by any means—but it does require the careful consideration of religion. Without the effort of thoughtfulness, morality becomes simply manners, to be laid aside when inconvenient or uncomfortable.

Religion gives us a language. Through religion we create forms and words with which to express and explore something we have *already* felt in our hearts. I attend a service at the church I joined several years ago (joined as a fearful stranger) and see a family: dozens of people I never see elsewhere, with whom I have no social contact except for church socials, and they are as intimate to me as the people with whom I live. I know their hearts, their pain; I know why they attend the service, too. And they know me. We use the language of our religion to abbreviate experience—to explain ourselves—and we use the small forms to express it. I feel held up by these people, supported as though I leaned on them as I walked. How could I fail to offer such a joy to my children?

Because I am raising my children in my own religion, we also share this vocabulary, free of embarrassment, in which to discuss intimate, disturbing, and wonderful possibilities. I see many parents who want their children to have religion leave them at the children's service and disappear for a few hours. They are giving their children a framework, a discipline and view, they refuse to give themselves. When one of my children suffers one of the peculiar torments of childhood—a bully, a broken toy, the discovery of a dead bird—we talk about it with certain words, words I've clarified in the past. I know it all stays somewhat mysterious to them; that's part of being young. A lot of it is mysterious to me, too—I have plenty of "why-me" moments in my life. Religion helps us to understand and then respond to the suffering in this sad world we inhabit, and the suffering within ourselves. We do our children a disservice if we fail to acknowledge *their* fear and suffering, as well, and give them tools.

"Spiritual realization is the whole point," writes Polly Berrien Berends, author of *Whole Child, Whole Parent*. "It is the driving force, heart's desire, and lifelong task of parent and child. It is the whole purpose of our being together, and the only workable way." It is "the whole point"—I like the solid strength of that statement. My oldest boy complains about his sack lunches—"All the other kids get Twinkies, why can't I?"—and I answer him with the pragmatic facts of nutrition, knowing he isn't really listening. My other son complains about money, equating toys with love, arguing that it is my purpose to make his life equivalent to those around him, to fill in the visible gaps. And again I answer in the immediate. My little girl stomps her toddler foot, screams with the indignation of the victimized as I carry her for a bath, a nap. As parents we do what we have to, knowing it won't be met with gratitude—we see the long view. But the whole point isn't nutrition, or money. It isn't even love. The point is in the doing—the selflessness. The point is, exactly, that there is to be no gratitude. When I remember this, I am really showing my children religion.

Not all parents find themselves with a strong faith. What then to teach the children? Doubtful parents, even unbelieving parents, can still offer children a forum. They can share their own journey, their own questions. Religion now is sometimes like sex to parents—questions about it embarrass us. We cultivate at times a disrespect for it, meant to show our courage. We are embarrassed most of all at being caught with our rational pants down, contemplating the non-quantifiable, engrossed in the immaterial while all around us our peers discuss the undeniably material world. One of the hardest phrases to utter in our lives is "I don't know." How much harder to say it to a wondering child, to raise our pants leg and show our clay feet for all to see.

It can be startling to hear my children state as absolute an idea I may secretly doubt. I haven't a rock-hard, unshakeable faith; I waver like most. This is good, in a way, because inflexible faith brooks no dissent and leaves no room for growth. But it is disconcerting to be reminded of my own convictions by my children. They are quick to scrutinize, dubious of excuses, and they gauge the worth of my words from my actions. Adherence to religious principles is no different from an adherence to more prosaic rules: don't lie, don't cheat, eat your vegetables before your dessert. But there is less room in my religious behavior for rationalization, or laziness. There are fewer exceptions.

The fact is, my children are quicker to forgive me than I am to return the favor. They are quicker to forgive me than I am to forgive myself. Perhaps because they are being raised in a different religion than I was, my children seem to suffer a little less guilt than I do. And because I tend to fall into guilt about my own less-than-perfect rendering of myself, I also tend to fall into blaming them for their own imperfections. Religious training can become an excessive demand for holiness. They come to devotion (when they come) naturally, without pretense; I come hungry, sometimes full of regret, a product of my own choices. An old line from the scriptures of my church says you must want the truth "like a drowning man wants air." There are days when I find it hard to breathe, when I feel lost, and desperately far from what I want to be. Then, if I'm willing to bow, I can gather my children's forgiveness and their innate perfection around me, and take comfort. And together we can practice the small forms.

The forms free me from that feeling of groundlessness. It is the proper restraint of certain impulses, and the free expression of others to practice ritual. Ritual is the cornerstone, the tangible, that which we can grasp. And ritual is something we *can* perfect—given enough practice. Another of our aphorisms: "The ceremony does itself." In real ritual, the participants need only get out of the way.

However brief or small, the things we do with reverence are significant, dependable, and stable. They are predictable, and tie us to a long history stretching behind and far ahead. There is in any ritual the sense that what you do in that moment, and whether you are able to do it properly and with care and attention, is *important*.

My church recently celebrated an important ceremony. Several members of the community were making a vow to a deeper commitment to religious training in the world. They were, in essence, being born into a new life, and those of us who had traveled with them so far were asked to be witnesses. It was a very long ceremony, with much repetition and much opportunity to reflect. There words spoken, the acts performed, were all quite familiar to me. So much of religious life is universal: the flame of a candle, the light, thin smoke of incense rising, the fresh color of a flower on an altar. And the form of this ceremony was universal, too: the brave venture of an individual into that rarefied world of practice, witnessed and approved by fellow travelers. When the ceremony was finished, and the solemnity eased at last, the priest clapped his hands and looked at the celebrants with happiness.

"We are about to embark on a great journey together," he told them. "And I'm glad you chose to go."

The import of religion, and its rituals, radiates into the hidden places, into our hearts and minds and the shadows of thought and feeling. Religion expands our framework, admits the impossibility of life's burdens, makes life bigger. That's what I want to give my children. When I let one child light the candle, ask another to say a verse, I am inviting them into a larger universe. Sometimes they giggle when we say the words. And then suddenly their backs straighten, and they sit still, as though gently and all of a sudden tugged upward.

The Geometry of Love

Margaret Visser

THE CLOSEST RELATIVE OF A CHURCH IS A THEATER, WHERE PEOPLE also come together to witness a scripted performance. There is a stage in a church, and seats for the audience; in both theater and church, people live together through a trajectory of the soul. They come to achieve contact with transcendence, to experience delight or recognition, to understand something they never understood before, to feel relief, to stare in amazement, to cry.

They want something that shakes them up or gives them peace.

Yet a theater is like a church—not the other way round. Drama grew out of religious performance (and never entirely left it) in a process wherein the play gradually separated itself from the crowd watching. The distance between watcher and watched is essential to theatrical experience (the word "theater" comes from the Greek *theatron*, a place for viewing), but people come together in a church not to view but to take part: "church" comes from the Greek *kyriakon*, "house of the Lord," a place of encounter between people and God.

But a church can go on "working" even when there is no performance and no crowd. A person can come into a silent church and respond to the building and its meaning. This can produce an experience as profoundly moving as that of attending a performance—something that cannot be said of visiting an empty theater.

A church stands in total opposition to the narrowing and flattening of human experience, the deviation into the trivial, that follow from antipathy towards meaning, and especially meaning held in common. Meaning is intentional: this building has been made in order to communicate with the people in it. A church is no place to practice aesthetic distance, to erase content and simply appreciate form. The building is trying to speak. Not listening to what it has to say is a form of barbarous inattention, like admiring a musical instrument while caring nothing for music.

CHURCHES ORIENT US. THE WORD "ORIENTATION" MEANS literally "turned towards the east" (*oriens* in Latin means "rising," and so where the sun rises). It is a word derived from church-building: many churches attend to the symbolism of the sun and its movement across the sky, having been built to conform with that cosmic pattern. The church is an invitation to travel, to stretch our souls and embrace the movement that time imposes upon our lives. Churches express time, but in terms of space. The use of space to "mean" time and movement is a church's way of preparing the visitor for its final objective, which is to point to infinity or the transcendent, where the oppositions perceived by our human senses are resolved, and all is understood to be one.

The Christian religion is itself founded on a vast contradiction; the habit of conflating opposites is indigenous to it. Christians believe that Jesus Christ is both God and human, an idea outrageous enough to have kept us argumentatively occupied for two thousand years. Some have thought Jesus was only a man, a very good person; some that he was human until he was baptized by John, at which point he became divine; some that he was never human at all but only appeared to be a man. To preserve the paradox and prevent the exclusion of one of the opposites, the institutional Church kept condemning such ideas—and many and ingenious were their formulations—as heresies. (The word "heresy" is from the Greek *haireo*, "I choose": heretics are people who choose to believe what they like, regardless of orthodoxy. "Orthodoxy," on the other hand, means literally "thinking in a straight line.") But in a sense there is always heresy, simply because Christians cannot—not easily, certainly not constantly, perhaps never—get their minds around the enormity of this central contradiction.

For well over the first thousand years of the Church's history, it was the deity of Christ that was emphasized. Christ was Pantokrator, the "All Powerful One," solemn and just, tranquil in his triumph because he had changed the world forever, and very male. Today, that has changed. Christians tend, at least in the West, to think of Jesus in his human aspect, as intensely human as it is possible to be, and as compassionate as the gentlest woman; some can scarcely fit his divinity into the picture. God himself (that is, Christ) is known to be suffering, even helpless in the face of the evil that humankind has freely chosen to commit. It can be hard these days to feel that God has "the whole world in his hand."

It is absolutely essential to the Christian message to accept that Christ is both God and human—equally, simultaneously, and always. It is indeed impossible to get one's mind around this paradox, yet that, and nothing less, is the crux (a truly Christian word) of everything in Christianity. A related contradiction is even harder to embrace. God is perceived on one hand as infinite, immense, the creator and sustainer of a universe, the universe whose unimaginable size we are only now beginning to discover; and on the other hand he is believed to be present in every single detail of his creation, to know and hold dear every atom, every speck of dust on every star and planet, to care about every blade of grass, every insect, every human being. To see Christ as both divine and human is to grasp two terms of a contradiction. God's spanning of one and many, huge and minuscule, this instant and always, here and everywhere, omnipotent and vulnerable is even further beyond human imagining—although mystics tell us that in privileged moments they have "seen" this truth. The profoundly Judeo-Christian idea that God is not a theorem or a pattern or a necessity, but a person—an *I*—takes us even further from common sense. But that is not all: Christians believe that this person ("I am who I am") is the root of love, and eternally loves us.

It takes only two words to say the most mind-boggling article of Christian belief there is: *God cares.*

ON MAY 8, 1373, A YOUNG WOMAN LAY DYING, AND SHE experienced God. She later recovered and lived, and wrote down what she had been shown when she met God, in a book called *Revelations of Divine Love.* Julian of Norwich received sixteen revelations in all; after the account of the last one she wrote: "Some of us believe that God is almighty, and may do everything; and that he is all wise, and can do everything; but that he is all love, and will do everything—there we draw back." No matter how horrendous the world's sufferings, no matter how triumphant wickedness looks, God revealed to Julian that "Sin is behovable [that is, necessary or inevitable], but all shall be well, and all shall be well, and all manner of thing shall be well."

God opened the series of revelations to Julian by showing her the universe. "And he showed me . . . a little thing, the size of a hazelnut, on the palm of my hand, round like a ball. I looked at it thoughtfully and wondered, 'What is this?' And the answer came, 'It is all that is made.' I marvelled that it continued to exist and did not suddenly disintegrate; it was so small. And again my mind supplied the answer, 'It exists, both now and for ever, because God loves it.'"

In the twelfth revelation God spoke to Julian in words I shall quote in Julian's original English with its high disdain for consistency in spelling: "I it am, I it am; I it am that is heyest; I it am that thou lovist; I it am that thou lykyst; I it am that thou servist; I it am that thou longyst; I it am that thou desyrist; I it am that thou menyst; I it am that is al; I it am that holy church prechyth and teachyth the; I it am that shewed me here to thee." "I it am that thou menyst," God said: "I am what you mean."

IN ANCIENT GREECE AND ROME A TEMPLE WAS A HOUSE FOR A GOD; it often stood on a hill, was raised on a podium, and was approached by steps. Around it was a precinct (literally "something with a belt, a cinch, tightly surrounding it"), a space where worshippers could gather; it was not for those who did not intend or who were not allowed to take part in the sacrifices and the feast that followed. The god's statue stood alone in the temple, in a windowless walled enclosure with a large door in front. The altar's place was in the precinct, not in the temple; when sacrifice was performed, the door to the god's enclosure was opened so that the deity could watch what was going on.

The sacrifice took place *pro fano*, in front of the *fanum*, the temple. (*Fanum* is from the Greek root *phan-*, meaning "show," as in "epiphany"; this was a place where the god revealed himself or herself.) What was outside the temple, pro fano, also could mean what was not holy, that is, merely—or sometimes appallingly—profane.

Christianity was born at the height of the Roman Empire; and when Christians eventually came to build their own churches, they built some of the first of them in Rome. So churches were heavily dependent, architecturally speaking, upon Roman technological and artistic know-how. Christian thinking grew within the matrix of ancient classical culture. But Christianity was born out of Jewish, not Greek or Roman, religion. The Jews also had a temple, a single building in Jerusalem that focused the nation and provided its ritual center. Within the "holy of holies," its sacred inner sanctum, this temple held for centuries the written Decalogue, or Ten Commandments, fruit of the encounter of Moses with God. The Jewish temple remembered and kept alive that revolutionary contact with the divine. Every Christian church remembers this temple, and often contains features that specifically echo its structure.

The Temple of Solomon in Jerusalem stood on a platform on a hill, in an area probably about fifty yards north of the present Dome of the Rock. Two free-standing bronze pillars rose at the top of the steps in front of the entrance, forming part of what was known as the *ulam*, a vestibule, porch, or narthex fifteen feet deep. From there the priests alone could enter an oblong space, the *hekal*, which is calculated to have been sixty feet long and thirty feet wide. The shape of this temple (similar as it is to the form of many a church today) had very ancient Middle Eastern roots. A hint of its antiquity can be glimpsed in the word *hekal*. It derives from Sumerian *egal*, "great house," referring to the house of a god or a king. (The great temple culture of the Sumerians, in modern Iraq, lasted from the fifth millennium to the twenty-fifth century B.C. Abraham had set out for Canaan from Ur, the temple city built by the Sumerians, probably during the early second millennium B.C.)

At the end of the hekal of Solomon's temple, opposite the entrance, was a square room, probably reached by climbing steps. It was a cubic space thirty feet by thirty feet by thirty feet, closed off with olive-wood doors sheathed in gold. This was the holy of holies, the Sancta Sanctorum, the *debir* in Hebrew. In this room— into which no one could enter but the high priest, and he on only one day in the year—stood the Ark containing the Covenant, watched over by two fifteen-foot-high golden cherubim, whose extended wings reached from wall to wall.

The temple stood for nearly four centuries, until the Babylonians under King Nebuchadnezzar invaded Jerusalem in 587 B.C. The temple was burned down, and the Ark of the Covenant disappeared. All the gold and precious metals from the treasury were stolen, and the survivors of the battle were deported to Babylon. Yet during the exile Ezekiel prophesied that the time would come when a new temple would rise. This time, however, the temple was symbolic, an embodiment in the mind of reunion and wholeness, of a return home from exile, of cohesion and order, harmony and balance: everything about this visionary temple was triumphantly symmetrical. Then the vision shows us a marvel. Ezekiel says that he was taken to see the fountain of water that would well up in the temple. This water became a stream, a river, a flood; it flowed into the Dead Sea and made the salt water fresh, so that it teemed with fish and water creatures. Trees grew in profusion around it, and people fished in the water and lived on the fruit of the trees and used the leaves for healing. The temple of Ezekiel's vision would turn the desert into Paradise, and death into life.

During the reign of King Herod I, (73–74 B.C.), the temple was fully rebuilt and refurbished. He doubled the size of the Temple Mount and created a podium thirty-six acres in extent to support a huge complex of buildings in addition to the temple. He re-created the menorah, the single gold candlestick that had graced the original tent in the wilderness, with seven branches holding cups in the form of open almond blossoms and lamps filled with pure olive oil. The veil that hung in front of the *debir*, or inner sanctum, also required in the Exodus prescription, was woven again in wool and linen of violet and scarlet and crimson, and worked with cherubim. A second, less magnificent curtain hung at the entrance to the temple from the *ulam*, or narthex.

This was the temple precinct that Jesus knew, though he would not have been allowed into the temple proper, because he was not a priest. The grandeur of the entire complex, its ancient story, deep significance, and profound roots should be present to anyone who hears that Jesus said he came both to fulfill the Law and to replace the temple—that indeed he *was* the real temple.

This temple in all its splendor was demolished by the Romans in the year 70, when they destroyed Jerusalem. On the Arch of Titus in Rome is depicted the scene of the Roman army returning in triumph with their booty, including what is apparently the gold candlestick, the menorah, from the temple. They ruthlessly wiped out the entire complex of buildings and pillaged its riches.

But the temple that Ezekiel foretold, the visionary temple, lived on.

There had been only one temple, the one in Jerusalem. But Jews had other shrines, and they also performed religious rituals at home, as they do to this day. In addition, they had meeting houses for prayer, meditation, and instruction. The Greek word for such a building is *synagogue*, a "coming together." It is still unknown when the first synagogues were conceived and built, but they represented a wholly new idea of communal religious observance. They were flourishing at the time of Jesus, who began his public ministry in one.

The form of the synagogue made reference to the temple. Then as now it was usually rectangular in plan, with a shrine-cupboard containing the rolls of the Scriptures set in one wall. It also had a raised platform in the midst, from which much of the service was conducted. A synagogue is for hearing and learning and discussing the Word: the history, traditions, prayers, and commentaries of the Jewish people. With the destruction of Jerusalem in A.D. 70, the Jews had to learn to do without the temple. The practice of sacrifice ceased. The many synagogues took over the role of religious centres.

IN THE EARLIEST DAYS AFTER THE DEATH OF JESUS, HIS FOLLOWERS continued to attend the still-standing temple. They also met together wherever a room large enough to contain the group could be found. The Jewish Scriptures remained their foundational book, as they still are for Christians today. For larger meetings they had the model of the synagogue, which was intensely familiar to them: almost all of them were Jews, and Jesus himself had been a Jew who was deeply committed to his people's religion.

The word "Christian" was not coined till some decades later, probably by Gentiles, and as a term of opprobrium. The first Christians continued simply to be Jews, or Judaizing Gentiles. However, they differed from their fellows in their belief that the Messiah, or "Anointed One" foretold, had come. He had turned out to be not a triumphant warrior or a master politician, but someone they had personally known, their own friend, a poor man, someone of immense personal power but of no account in the world of public affairs, an innocent man, utterly committed to nonviolence, who had suffered the death of a criminal. Such a Messiah could not have been more unexpected (although, in the Christian interpretation, his character had in fact been foretold in the Jewish Scriptures). For Christians, Jesus and none other was the Messiah, *Christos*, "Anointed One" in Greek. Not only that, but they also believed Jesus was no longer dead; he was still with them. In Jesus, they came to be convinced, God himself had become human.

The temple at Jerusalem is very much a part of the narrative concerning Jesus in the four Gospels. But the actual temple, from a Christian point of view, was always destined to pass away. Indeed, at least three of the Gospels were written after the temple had been destroyed (that of Mark may have been the exception). The temple, however, was an embodiment of the story of God's chosen people and a sign or "type" of what was to come; for Christians it was subsumed in Jesus and in the Church. Christians believed that Jesus was what the temple had anticipated; he was the "presence of God" that it promised.

The climactic end of Jesus' life began with his outrage at the people's lack of respect for "his father's house," the temple. (The rage of Jesus recalls that of Moses when he found his people worshipping the golden calf.) So important was this incident in the memory of his disciples that all of the Gospels record it, and John places it very near the beginning of his account. It took place in the outer esplanade of the temple, the only area where Gentiles were allowed. There Greek and Roman currency was exchanged for Jewish and Tyrian shekels, and animals and birds were sold for sacrifice. Even Jesus' own parents, when they had presented him as an infant at the temple in accordance with the laws of Israel, had changed their money for shekels and bought birds for the mandated sacrifice. But in his rage Jesus pushed over the tables, made a whip of cords, and thrashed the money vendors and the salesmen out of the "den of thieves" they had created. It was shocking behavior, and clearly arose from his sense of reverence for God's holy place.

Immediately after this incident Jesus said to the people who remonstrated with him, "Destroy this temple, and in three days I will raise it up." They were furious, and contemptuous of his folly; the charges at his trial included the blasphemy of this remark. But they had not understood the riddle. By "this temple" Jesus meant himself; he was saying that he had replaced the temple. His kingdom was not to be protected and privileged by means of purity. He himself was not sacrosanct: his body would be agonizingly pierced, and his heart pierced again after his death. He saw to it that everybody could have access to him by means of the endlessly reproduced bread that is his body, "this temple." No one would be excluded, unless people wished to exclude themselves. And he would "raise the temple up" from death, in three days.

Matthew relates that when Jesus died on the cross, "the veil of the temple was torn in two from top to bottom." Henceforth, Christians believed, the holy of holies would lie open for all to approach it; salvation history was beginning a new era.

CHRISTIANITY IS THE NAME OF A CONTINUING ENDEAVOR TO TAKE up and live the implications of the life and death of Christ, of the belief that in him God has broken into human history. Within the family of institutions that try to remember the insights they receive from him, there are many cultures, many tastes and traditions, many differences of attitude and emphasis. These are expressed especially vividly in the buildings they occupy.

Some Christians prefer to worship God at home and in private, or with other people in something ad hoc—under some trees, say, or in a garage or a shed or a school basement. And indeed, according to the Gospels, Jesus instituted the Eucharist in a dining room borrowed from a friend, and foreshadowed this event in the multiplication of loaves and fishes in an open field and in the hills beside a lake. When Christians meet in buildings the architectural possibilities range widely, from the austere to the exuberant. Everything is to be found, from the simplest halls or meeting houses, to modern churches that may be purely functional or make dramatic "statements," to imposing, fortresslike stone buildings, perhaps accommodating here and there a minimum of artistic heightening, to magnificent and elaborate Gothic cathedrals and their progeny, to luxuriously decorated churches, to Baroque edifices revelling in deliberate excess, to garish constructions choked with statuary and clutter.

But why have churches at all? The very idea of having such a thing as a church building must be questioned, given Christianity's founding story. For a Christian, not to ask this question, or even to feel comfortable about his or her answer, is to deny something that lies at the heart of Christianity. God, or the truth, is not confined to the Church, let alone by church buildings. Every Christian should remain deeply suspicious of churches—both as buildings and as institutions; it is part of following Christ.

The paradox is there from the beginning. For example, when Jesus hounded the money-changers out of the temple, he wanted people to respect God's house—even as he proposed to replace it. Churches can be confining and deadening—and churches may liberate and enliven. Buildings are unnecessary—but needed. Churches remain—but they remain in order to keep alive a message that is all about movement, about hope and change. In short, a Christian church seems to be—and quite consciously is—a contradiction in terms.

THE EUCHARIST IS THE FOCAL POINT, THE LIFE AND HEART OF THE whole. It is the point of encounter between God and humanity in Christ. And it is available to everyone.

In the Eucharist, God—infinite vastness—enters into the person who eats this bread and drinks this cup. It is as food and drink—the object for human beings of endlessly renewed desire, necessary, simple, ordinary, to be broken and shared, of external matter that becomes internal, and which then turns into the very substance of the eater—that the Christian God of love sacramentally gives himself to human beings. In spatial and temporal terms, always and everywhere become, in the Eucharist, one with here and now.

The altar where the Mass is said and the bread and wine of the Eucharist itself combine to express Christ's death—and his life. It is in order to remember that death that the Eucharistic table in a Catholic church is referred to as an altar, and is frequently made in the shape of one. (The Eucharist, in fact, does not require an altar, or even a table—any surface will do.)

The idea of sacrifice, of killing a creature in order to achieve both human togetherness and an encounter with the divine, has been found everywhere on earth; a raised slab on which a sacrifice is performed is known as an altar. Christianity, however, rejected blood sacrifice; this was in its time one of the most revolutionary aspects of the new religion. According to Christians, mediating sacrificial victims were no longer needed, for in the death of Jesus, God himself had become the victim, once and for all.

It was the ultimate epiphany of his love: God had suffered as a victim suffers, and continues this solidarity with all victims. Christ's death at the hands of human beings definitively revealed the horror inherent in violence and made every subsequent act of violence an outrage. Scapegoating and violence continue in the world, but never again can they escape the light that reveals them for what they are.

The altar used as a Eucharistic table in a church is symbolic. It remembers, first of all, the ancient sacrificial altar at the Jewish temple. The altar, which stood outside both a pagan temple and the Jewish temple, is brought right into the center of a Christian church. It becomes the Christian holy of holies, the point of encounter between God and the group of people seeking him, between God and individual human beings.

THE EUCHARIST—THE CENTRAL RITE OF CHRISTIANITY—NOT only symbolizes but also enacts sharing in love. In this ritual a number of great oppositions are articulated and the barriers dividing them collapsed: God and humankind; the group and the individual; death and life; spirit and body; then and now; here, elsewhere, and everywhere; eternal and temporal; and even meaning and fact ("This is my body").

The first Christians met in private houses, around ordinary tables in dining rooms, needing only bread and wine for their central epiphanic ritual. The elements of the Eucharist are indeed simple—but the meanings encompassed are vast. The action is intended to express union with God: oneness with what is eternally beyond and greater than human capacity. Eating, even before sex, is biological evolution's first step towards transcendence in the animal species because it initiates physical openness to and need for the Other. For Catholic Christians, the Eucharist is God's gift of himself to humankind; and the ultimate sacramental mystery of love again takes the form of eating and drinking.

The altar remembers the central belief of Christianity, that from Christ's cruel death, new hope and the possibility of liberation were born for humanity. It concretely embodies the psalmist's poetic metaphor, which Jesus took to mean himself: "It was the stone rejected by the builders that became the cornerstone," the stone upon which the whole edifice depends. Simon, son of Jonah, himself nicknamed Peter, "the stone," was later to comment on the relationship between the crucifixion of Jesus (his "rejection") and his status now as "the cornerstone" of the new view of the world. People who do not believe that Jesus is the Christ foretold will not think him a "cornerstone" at all, Peter wrote; they will find him a "stumbling-block." The latter expression in Greek is *petra skandalou*, the origin of the English word "scandal"; it means a stone that people fall over. Every altar in a Catholic church must either be of natural stone or contain a stone element in the top of it, in order to recall this scandalous claim.

WHENEVER CHRISTIANS WANT TO REBEL AGAINST THE ORGANIZED Church with its hierarchies and traditions, against the prestige inherent in beautiful buildings, against having to fit into structures instead of feeling free to create and expand into the new—then they tend to complain about churches. After a while, if they continue to meet at all, they prefer bare halls, basements, living rooms, and garages in which to pray together: in these they feel they are being purer, more energetic, approaching closer to their roots. It is a true and faithful option, and often a necessary one for those who choose it.

On the other hand, a well-made church that survives such times of purgation can offer almost limitless riches for the imagination, and therefore for the soul. It is, after all, entirely natural for human beings to find inspiration in direct contact with their past, with what has gone into creating their loves. And people who have access to a spiritual tradition commonly know at a profound (though not necessarily conscious) level how to "read" a church, and can respond to it instinctively. Deliberately to forgo such pleasure and enrichment is an ascetic feat, and one to be undertaken only with full knowledge of the reasons for it and the risks and losses involved.

For anyone who is not spiritually allergic to churches, to walk into a beautiful church is to encounter understanding, to hear echoes of the soul's own experiences of epiphany. Such stimulus and concurrence need not involve anything theological. It can be a matter simply of sunlight striking through colored glass and dappling the wall opposite, of the smell of flowers and lingering hints of incense, of the silent cold of stone, of movements of the soul that respond directly to columns, arches, domes, coloring, and carving, or to the memory of the people who have filled this building in the past. I myself find it an invariable satisfaction just to see the dark entrance of a church (open!), even on a quick drive through an unknown town. It's a hole in the hard walls of the rackety everyday, a reassurance that, thanks to the care and attention of my fellow human beings, a place has been made ready for silent contact with something enormous, something present, for anyone who wants it.

Dreaming God's Dream

ARCHBISHOP JOHN VLAZNY

WHAT IS A MATURE CATHOLIC FAITH? THIS IS A VERY GOOD question for me to ponder, having achieved my sixty-fifth birthday this year. One would think that at such a milestone a certain level of maturity in one's relationship with God would have been achieved.

I wonder.

Long ago Jesus Christ came among us preaching the kingdom of God. Those around Him, even the brightest and the best, right away asked, *what's in it for me?* Not a very mature question, but a wholly understandable one. In my judgment, however, a mature Catholic faith has been achieved when that question is no longer on the table.

I admit that following Jesus and helping Him build God's kingdom brings many blessings my way. But good times, personal satisfaction, much acclaim, and lots of success are the desirable prizes of adolescence—and so are these things the prizes of an adolescent faith. A mature Catholic faith reaches far beyond one's personal comfort zones.

A mature Catholic faith is interested in keeping the focus much more on God and other people, much less on one's self. The mature Catholic is not dissuaded from the task of kingdom-building even though the personal rewards seem minimal (at best) and the beneficiaries unremarkable and unknowable.

LAST SUMMER I HAD A CONVERSATION WITH A YOUNG MAN WHO was entering the seminary to prepare for the priesthood in our archdiocese. After our conversation it occurred to me that our partnership in ordained church ministry would not be especially long-lasting. I would be expected to retire a couple of years after he would be ordained. Why bother? How would he ever help me carry out my duties as pastor of this local church? My adolescent faith—never something I've grown completely out of—was raising its selfish head once again.

Continuing the mission of Jesus Christ, building the kingdom of God here on earth, promoting the works of peace and justice— all these and more are long-term tasks. It's great to be part of them but the results we desire won't be achieved in our lifetime. In fact, the eventual accomplishment of such momentous challenges is probably far beyond our imagining. Yet, as disciples in mission, the situation is not uniquely our own.

Recently I learned about an ongoing scientific project to make the planet Mars habitable for humans. Those who are investing themselves in the project see it as a task with a duration of a millennium. Just think how unselfish a person must be to invest himself or herself in something so large and prolonged that that he or she and all foreseeable progeny will never live to witness its success. Yet people in the scientific world are willing to do this.

The same must be true for the mature Christian. Mature Christians do indeed invest themselves in the works of justice and peace so that one day all people will live in solidarity as sisters and brothers in one worldwide family. The mature Christian is both patient and persevering, but also humble enough to acknowledge that the ultimate success of such a mission can only be achieved with the help of God.

What, then, is a mature Catholic faith? Mature Catholic people in the three local churches where I have been privileged to serve taught me that such a faith is one that looks to serving God and others, yet easily takes or leaves whatever is self-serving in the process. A mature Catholic faith, in short, takes God's dream for us and makes it our own.

Santa Teresa

TERRY TEMPEST WILLIAMS

ON THE TRAIN TO AVILA, TAMARISKS ARE IN BLOOM. PINES. Junipers. Arid shrub country pocketed with boulders. Magpies. Poppies. The *meseta* or plateau country of central Spain looks much like my home in the American southwest.

The medieval walls surrounding the *ciudad antigua*, the old city, of Avila are the threshold to the world of Santa Teresa in the early sixteenth century. Even though the walls were built miraculously five hundred years earlier by nineteen hundred men in nine years after the town had been reclaimed from the Moors, it is Teresa's presence that lingers.

Santa Teresa sits outside her city, reposed in white marble, her gaze directed over her right shoulder, a plume pen in her right hand, her left hand open to the Mysteries.

Hundreds of swifts circle her. Pink, white, and yellow roses flourish against the stone wall. Someone has left a bouquet of wild-flowers at her feet. Overhead three storks fly toward the bell tower del Carmen where they nest. Did Santa Teresa know these birds, these mediators between heaven and earth? These swifts and storks must have swayed her thinking. Surely the Holy Spirit appears in more incarnations than doves.

TO WHOM DO I PRAY?

A Spanish woman sits in the row across from me in the Iglesia de Santa Teresa reciting her prayers in whispers as she rotates each bead of her rosary through her fingers. Her hands are folded beneath her chin. She alternates her prayers with the reading of scriptures.

To whom do I pray?

I kneel before the statue of Santa Teresa, gilded and animated by the soft light in this small dark alcove. Her right hand is outstretched as though she were about to touch Spirit, her left hand covers her heart.

I close my eyes and listen.

After many minutes of silence, what comes into my mind is the phrase, "wet not dry."

I close my eyes tighter and concentrate more deeply, let these words simply pass through as one does with distractions in meditation. Again, the words, "wet not dry." The woman across the aisle from me is weeping. Her private utterings, "para ti," for you, are audible. I open my eyes feeling little emotion and look down at the worn tiles beneath my feet. The Spanish woman faces the Saint, bows, crosses herself and leaves.

Wondering if I should be here at all, I try once again to pray. In the stillness, the phrase returns.

All I can hear in the sanctity of this chapel is what sounds at best like a cheap antiperspirant jingle. Filled with shame, I look up at Santa Teresa's face.

LATER THAT AFTERNOON, I STEADY MYSELF BY SITTING BENEATH AN old cottonwood tree, similar to the ones I have sat under a hundred times in the desert. I open Santa Teresa's autobiography, *The Life of Saint Teresa of Avila by Herself* and randomly turn to a page, ". . . and God converted the dryness of my soul into a great tenderness." I turn another page, "Only once in my life do I remember asking Him for consolation and that was when I was very dry . . ." And another, "It is my opinion that though a soul may seem to be deriving some immediate benefit when it does anything to further itself in this prayer of union, it will in fact very quickly fall again, like buildings without foundations . . . Remain calm in times of dryness."

Unknown to me, Santa Teresa's book articulates "the Four Waters of Prayer." She says simply that wetness brings us "to a recollected state." A well. A spring. A fountain. To drink deeply from the Spirit and quench the aridity of the soul to retrieve, revive, and renew our relationship with God.

Where are my tears? Where is the rain? I ask myself. "I am now speaking of that rain that comes down abundantly from heaven to soak and saturate the whole garden."

The leaves of the cottonwood tree shield me from the heat as I read her *Confessions* slowly: "Who is this whom all my faculties thus obey? Who is it that in a moment sheds light amidst such great darkness, who softens a heart that seemed to be of stone and sheds the water of gentle tears where for so long it had seemed to be dry? Who gives these desires? Who gives this courage? What have I been thinking of? What am I afraid of?"

The smell of lavender and rosemary collide in the garden. Something breaks open in me. What might it mean to honor thirst before hunger and joy before obligation?

Un botela de agua. Necissito un botela de agua. These are the first words out of my mouth this morning as I awaken from a dream.

THE MONASTERIO DE ENCARNACION, A DIGNIFIED GRANITE fortress north of the Wall, is not far from the parador where I am staying. In 1534, Santa Teresa walked through these doors when she was twenty years old. It is closed. I sit on the stone steps outside the corridor. *Hace calor.* I settle in the shade and read more of Santa Teresa's words, "All its joys came in little sips."

As I continue to read her autobiography, the mystic writes about women and the importance of discretion in speaking of one's spiritual experiences, the need to share with others of like mind for solace and safety, reflection, and inspiration.

Joseph Smith believed so fully in Santa Teresa's visions, that he had himself sealed with the Carmelite nun in "the everlasting covenant of marriage." He recognized her as a spiritual soulmate, trusting that revelations from God have been and will be continuous through time, that the truth is soul-wrenching, having said himself that he shared only a hundredth of what he saw when the heaven opened up to him. Schooled in the hermetic traditions of Santa Teresa's time, he might have felt as though they were contemporaries, sympathetic to her roving states of mind.

She speaks of her progress in prayer, "It seemed to me that there must either be something very good or something extremely bad about it. I was quite certain that my experiences were supernatural. . . ." Santa Teresa sought the help of a learned cleric. Many had said she was possessed by the devil. He did not. He encouraged her to find her own path of revelation, "to trust oneself in God, in Truth."

I CLOSE THE BOOK FEELING WEAK, LIGHT-HEADED, PERHAPS BECAUSE of the heat, perhaps because of the intensity of Santa Teresa's story: a child who at the age of ten vowed to be a nun but at age fourteen blossomed into a vibrant young woman enraptured by the sensory pleasures of the world, gifted in poetry and literature.

She fell tumultuously in love and was so frightened by her own sexuality that she confessed to her father, who immediately sent her to the convent. There, struggling with the disciplined life set by the nuns against her own instinctive nature, she succumbed to violent seizures and bouts of hysteria that eventually left her paralyzed for years, seized by the darkest of visions, unable to move, her pain barely tolerable. She denounced all medical treatments and relied solely on prayer, never giving up hope of being healed. At one point, deep in a coma mistaken for death, the nuns dug a grave for her. And then the miraculous day arrived. In 1540, she awoke to find her arms and legs no longer paralyzed. She had successfully passed through her journey through Hell. Teresa de Avila stood up and walked. It was proclaimed a miracle, a cure that reached the masses whereby people from surrounding villages came to see the nun who God had healed.

Her life from that point forward was a testament of austere devotion and simplicity, be she never gave up her pen.

INSIDE THE MONASTERIO, THERE ARE RELICS: A WOODEN LOG which Santa Teresa used as a pilow; a small statue of Christ "covered with wounds" which is said to have been very important to her spiritual awakening of compassion and sorrow; a statue of Saint Joseph who taught her how to pray. The nuns have passed down the story that this statue used to talk to Santa Teresa. When she left on her travels she would leave him on the prioress' chair. Upon her return, he would tell her everything that had gone on in her absence. The key to her cell where she lived for twenty-seven years begs to be turned. Turn the key. Santa Teresa's hands open the door. Downstairs, there is a tiny revolving door made of oak. It was the only access the nuns had with the outside world, sending messages out with one turn and receiving them with another in silence.

I descend further into the stark parlor where San Juan de la Cruz and Santa Teresa were *suspendido en extasis,* lifted in ecstacy. Once again, I sit quietly. The word *casado* comes into my mind, marriage, a prayer of union, a state of oneness with God and with whom we confide our bodies. The Divine Lover. In these moments of pure union, body, soul, and spirit fuse. Ecstacy. Elevation. Suspension.

THE BELLS OF THE MONASTERIO DE LA ENCARNACION BEGIN ringing. In the courtyard, two young girls are singing, one is playing the guitar, the other is clapping with her eyes closed. I walk down the road to the plaza where there is a fountain bubbling up from a stone basin and sit down.

Teenagers play in the pool below the fountain. They flirt and splash each other, then the young men and women, soaked, hoist each other up and over the stone wall and disappear. A man interrupted their frolicking to fill two jugs tied together by a rope that he swings over his neck.

The small plaza is quiet. I walk to the fountain and wash my face and hands and arms. The water is cold and invigorating. I wash my face again.

An old man with a black beret dressed in a white shirt with an olive green cardigan and grey slacks comes to the fountain carrying a plastic sack with two gallon water jugs. He is wearing blue canvas slippers.

I learn he is from one of the outlying pueblos in the mountains, that he makes this journey once a week to collect water for his wife from this particular fountain. He tells me this is *la funta del Santa Teresa . . . muy espiritu.* His wife is especially devoted to Santa Teresa de Avila. She believes this water restores the spirit and all manner of ailments. He invites me to drink the water with him.

I watch him walk carefully over the uneven cobbles and cannot begin to guess his age. He is a small and handsomely weathered man. He lifts his weary legs over the steps of the fountain, stoops down and then with great deliberation begins to fill each bottle. He fills one with about an inch of water, shakes the bottle then pours it out, filling it the second time as he sits down on the stone ledge above the spout. The old man enjoys several sips, wipes his mouth with the back of his hand and fills it again.

Joining him from below, I cup my hands below the running water and drink.

The old man gestures to one of the two bottles he has just painstakingly filled. It rests on the ledge like a prism separating lights the sun shines through.

At first, I do not understand. Perhaps he is offering me another drink?

Gracias, pero no.

He persists.

Para mi?

He nods. He hands me one of his bottles. I hardly know what to do. The old man had walked so far for this water. What will his wife say when he returns home to the mountains with only one bottle? How to receive this gift? What can I give him in return? I hold the jug of water close and feel its refreshment even against my skin.

Gracias, senor, para tu regalo.

De nada.

The old man nods and smiles and slowly shifts his weight on his right hand to ease himself up. He bends down and puts the other bottle in his bag.

After he is gone, I look back toward the fountain. "For tears gain everything; and one kind of water attracts another . . . "

Making Religion

EDWARD O. WILSON

RELIGIONS ARE ANALOGOUS TO SUPERORGANISMS. THEY HAVE A life cycle. They are born, they grow, they compete, they reproduce, and, in the fullness of time, most die. In each of these phases religions reflect the human organisms that nourish them.

Successful religions typically begin as cults, which then increase in power and inclusiveness until they achieve tolerance outside the circle of believers. At the core of each religion is a creation myth, which explains how the world began and the chosen people—those prescribing to the belief system—arrived at its center. There is often a mystery, a set of secret instructions and formulas available only to those who have worked their way to a higher state of enlightenment. The medieval Jewish cabala, the trigradal system of Freemasonry, and the carvings on Australian Aboriginal spirit sticks are examples of such arcana. Power radiates from the center, gathering converts and binding followers to the group. Sacred places are designated where the gods can be importuned, rites observed, and miracles witnessed. The devotees of the religion compete as a tribe with those of other religions. They harshly resist the dismissal of their beliefs by others. They venerate sacrifice in defense of the religion.

The tribalistic roots of moral reasoning and those of religion are similar and may be identical. Religious rites, as evidenced by burial ceremonies, are very old. In the late Paleolithic of Europe, bodies were sometimes placed in shallow graves sprinkled with ochre and blossoms, and it is easy to imagine ceremonies performed there that invoked spirits and gods. But, as theoretical deduction and the evidence suggest, the primitive elements of moral behavior are far older. Religion arose on an ethical foundation, and it has probably always been used in one manner or another to justify moral codes.

The formidable influence of the religious drive is based on far more, however, than just the validation of morals. A great subterranean river of the mind, it also gathers strength from a broad spread of other tributary emotions. Foremost among them is the survival instinct. "The fear of death," as the Roman poet Lucretius said, "is the first thing on earth to make the gods." Our conscious minds hunger for a more lasting existence. If we cannot have everlasting life of the body, then absorption into some immortal whole will serve. *Anything* will serve, so long as it gives the individual meaning and somehow stretches out into eternity that swift passage of the mind and spirit lamented by St. Augustine as the short day of time.

The understanding and control of life is another source of religious power. Doctrine draws on the same creative springs as science and the arts, its aim being the extraction of order from the chaos of the material world. To explain the meaning of life it spins mythic narratives of the tribal history that populate the cosmos with protective spirits and gods. The existence of the supernatural, if accepted, testifies to the existence of the world beyond so desperately desired.

Religion is also empowered powerfully by tribalism. The shamans and priests implore us, *Trust in the sacred rituals, become part of the immortal force, you are one of us. As your life unfolds, each step has mystic significance that we who love you will mark with a solemn rite of passage, the last to be performed when you enter that second world free of pain and fear.*

If the religious mythos did not exist in a culture, it would be quickly invented, and in fact it has been everywhere, thousands of times. Such inevitability is the mark of instinctual behavior in any species. That is, even when learned, it is guided toward certain states by emotion-driven rules of mental development. To call religion instinctive is not to suppose any particular part of its mythos is untrue, only that its sources run deeper than ordinary habit and are in fact hereditary, urged into birth through biases in mental development encoded in the genes.

There is a hereditary selective advantage to membership in a powerful group united by devout belief and purpose. Even when individuals subordinate themselves and risk death in common cause, their genes are more likely to be transmitted to the next generation than are those of competing groups who lack equivalent resolve.

The mathematical models of population genetics suggest the following rule in the evolutionary origin of such altruism. If the reduction of survival and reproduction of individuals due to genes for altruism is more than offset by the increased probability of survival of the group due to the altruism, the altruism genes will rise in frequency throughout the entire population of competing groups.

Much if not all religious behavior could have arisen from evolution by natural selection. The theory fits crudely. Propitiation and sacrifice, which are near-universals of religious practice, are acts of submission to a dominant being. They are one kind of a dominance hierarchy, which is a general trait of organized mammalian societies. Like humans, animals use elaborate signals to advertise and maintain their rank in the hierarchy. The details vary among species but also have consistent similarities across the board, as the following two examples will illustrate.

In packs of wolves the dominant animal walks erect and "proud," stiff-legged, deliberately paced, with head, tail, and ears up, while freely and casually staring at others. In the presence of rivals, the dominant animal bristles its pelt while curling its lips to show teeth, and it takes first choice in food and space. A subordinate uses opposite signals. It turns away from the dominant individual while lowering its head, ears, and tail, and it keeps its fur sleeked and teeth covered. It grovels and slinks, and it yields food and space when challenged.

In troops of rhesus monkeys, the alpha male of the troop is remarkably similar in mannerisms to a dominant wolf. He keeps his head and tail up, walks in a deliberate, "regal" manner while casually staring at others. He climbs nearby objects to maintain height above his rivals. When challenged he stares hard at the opponent with mouth open—signaling aggression, not surprise—and sometimes slaps the ground with open palms to signal his readiness to attack. The male or female subordinate affects a furtive walk, holding its head and tail down, turning away from the alpha and other higher ranked individuals. It keeps its mouth shut except for a fear grimace, and when challenged makes a cringing retreat. It yields space and food and, in the case of males, estrous females.

Behavioral scientists from another planet would notice immediately the semiotic resemblance between animal dominance behavior on the one hand and human obeisance to religious and civil authority on the other. They would point out that the most elaborate rites of obeisance are directed at the gods, the hyper-dominant members of the human group. And they would conclude, correctly, that in baseline social behavior, not just in anatomy, *Homo sapiens* has only recently diverged in evolution from a nonhuman primate stock.

Countless studies of animal species, with instinctive behavior unobscured by cultural elaboration, have shown that membership in dominance orders pays off in survival and lifetime reproductive success. That is true not just for the dominant individuals, but for the subordinates as well. Membership in either class gives animals better protection against enemies and better access to food, shelter, and mates than does solitary existence. Furthermore, subordination in the group is not necessarily permanent. Dominant individuals weaken and die, and as a result some of the underlings advance in rank and appropriate more resources.

It would be surprising to find that modern humans had managed to erase the old mammalian genetic programs and to devise other means of distributing power. All the evidence suggests that they have not. True to their primate heritage, people are easily seduced by confident, charismatic leaders, especially males. That predisposition is strongest in religious organizations. Cults form around such leaders. Their power grows if they can persuasively claim special access to the supremely dominant, typically male figure of God. As cults evolve into religions, the image of the supreme being is reinforced by myth and liturgy. In time the authority of the founders and their successors is graven in sacred texts. Unruly subordinates, known as "blasphemers," are squashed.

The symbol-forming human mind, however, never stays with raw apish satisfaction in any emotion realm. It strives to build cultures that are maximally rewarding in every dimension. In religion there is ritual and prayer to contact the supreme being directly, consolation from coreligionists to soften otherwise unbearable grief, explanations of the unexplainable, and an oceanic sense of communion with the larger whole.

Communion is the key, and hope rising from it eternal; out of the dark night of the soul there is the prospect of a spiritual journey to the light. For a special few the journey can be taken in this life. The mind reflects in certain ways in order to reach ever higher levels of enlightenment until finally, when no further progress is possible, it enters a mystical union with the whole. Within the great religions, such enlightenment is expressed by the Hindu samadhi, Buddhist Zen satori, Sufi fana, Taoist wu-wei, and Pentecostal Christian rebirth. Something like it is also experienced by hallucinating preliterate shamans. What all these celebrants evidently feel (as I have once to some degree as a reborn evangelical) is hard to put in words, but Willa Cather came as close as possible in a single sentence. "That is happiness," her fictional narrator says in *My Antonia*, "to be dissolved into something complete and great."

Of course that is happiness, to find the godhead, or to enter the wholeness of Nature, or otherwise to grasp and hold on to something ineffable, beautiful, and eternal. Millions seek it. They feel otherwise lost, adrift in a life without ultimate meaning. They enter established religions, succumb to cults, dabble in New Age nostrums. They push *The Celestine Prophecy* and other junk pretenses of enlightenment onto the bestseller lists.

Perhaps, as I believe, it can all eventually be explained as brain circuitry and deep history. But this is not a subject that even the most hardened empiricist should presume to trivialize. The idea of the mystical union is an authentic part of the human spirit. It has occupied humanity for millennia, and it raises questions of utmost seriousness for transcendentalists and scientists alike.

No one has described the true journey with greater clarity than the great Spanish mystic Saint Teresa of Avila:

> *O my King, seeing that I am now, while writing this, still under the power of this heavenly madness . . . grant, I beseech Thee, that all those with whom I may have to converse may become mad through Thy love, or let me converse with none, or order it that I may have nothing to do in the world, or take me away from it.*

In her "fourth state" of prayer Teresa attains mystical union:

> *There is no sense of anything, only fruition . . . the senses are all occupied in this function in such a way that not one of them is at liberty. . . . The soul while thus seeking after God, is conscious, with a joy excessive and sweet, that it is, as it were, utterly fainting away in a trance; breathing, and all the bodily strength fail it. The soul is dissolved into that of God, and with the union at last comes comprehension of the graces bestowed by Him.*

For many the urge to believe in transcendental existence and immortality is overpowering. Transcendentalism, especially when reinforced by religious faith, is psychically full and rich; it feels somehow *right*. In comparison empiricism seems sterile and inadequate. In the quest for ultimate meaning, the transcendentalist route is much easier to follow. That is why, even as empiricism is winning the mind, transcendentalism continues to win the heart. In the United States there are fifteen million Southern Baptists, the largest denomination favoring literal interpretation of the Christian Bible, but only five thousand members of the American Humanist Association, the leading organization devoted to secular and deistic humanism.

Still, if history and science have taught us anything, it is that passion and desire are not the same as truth. The human mind evolved to believe in the gods. It did not evolve to believe in biology. Acceptance of the supernatural conveyed a great advantage throughout prehistory, when the brain was evolving. Thus it is in sharp contrast to biology, which was developed as a product of the modern age and is not underwritten by genetic algorithms. The uncomfortable truth is that the two beliefs are not factually compatible. As a result those who hunger for both intellectual and religious truth will never completely achieve both.

Meanwhile, theology tries to resolve the dilemma by evolving sciencelike toward abstraction. The gods of our ancestors were divine human beings. The Egyptians, as Herodotus noted, represented them as Egyptian (often with body parts of Nilotic animals), and the Greeks represented them as Greeks. The great contribution of the Hebrews was to combine the entire pantheon into a single person, Yahweh—a patriarch appropriate to desert tribes—and to intellectualize His existence. No graven images were allowed. In the process, they rendered the divine presence less tangible. And so in biblical accounts it came to pass that no one, not even Moses approaching God in the burning bush, could look upon His face. In time the Jews were prohibited even from pronouncing His true full name. Nevertheless, the idea of a theistic God, omniscient, omnipotent, and closely involved in human affairs, has persisted to the present day as the dominant religious image of Western culture.

During the Enlightenment a growing number of liberal Judaeo-Christian theologians, wishing to accommodate theism to a more rationalist view of the material world, moved away from God as a literal person. Baruch Spinoza, the preeminent Jewish philosopher of the seventeenth century, visualized the deity as a transcendent substance present everywhere in the universe. *Deus sive natura*, God or nature, he declared, they are interchangeable. For his philosophical pains he was banished from Amsterdam under a comprehensive anathema, combining all curses in the book. The risk of heresy notwithstanding, the depersonalization of God has continued steadily into the modern era. For Paul Tillich, one of the most influential Protestant theologians of the twentieth century, the assertion of the existence of God-as-person is not false; it is just meaningless. Among many of the most liberal contemporary thinkers, the denial of a concrete divinity takes the form of process theology. Everything in this most extreme of ontologies is part of a seamless and endlessly complex web of unfolding relationships: God is manifest in everything.

SCIENTISTS, THE ROVING SCOUTS OF THE EMPIRICIST MOVEMENT, are not immune to the idea of God. Those who favor it often lean toward some form of process theology. They ask this question: When the real world of space, time, and matter is well enough known, will that knowledge reveal the Creator's presence? Their hopes are vested in the theoretical physicists who pursue the grail of the final theory, the Theory of Everything, T.O.E., a system of interlocking equations that describe all that can be learned of the forces of the physical universe. T.O.E. is a "beautiful" theory, as Steven Weinberg has called it in his important essay *Dreams of a Final Theory*. Beautiful because it will be elegant, expressing the possibility of unending complexity with minimal laws, and symmetric, because it will hold invariant through all space and time. And inevitable, meaning that once stated no part can be changed without invalidating the whole.

The prospect of a final theory by the most mathematical of scientists might seem to signal the approach of a new religious awakening. Stephen Hawking, yielding to the temptation in *A Brief History of Time* (1988), declared that this scientific achievement would be the ultimate triumph of human reason, "for then we would truly know the mind of God."

Well, I doubt it. Physicists have already laid in place a large part of the final theory. We know the trajectory; we can see roughly where it is headed. But there will be no religious epiphany, at least none recognizable to the authors of Holy Scripture. Science has taken us very far from the personal God who once presided over Western Civilization. It has done little to satisfy our instinctual hunger so poignantly expressed by the psalmist:

Man liveth his days like a shadow, and he disquieteth himself in vain with prideful delusions; his treasures, he knoweth not who shall gather them. Now, Lord, what is my comfort? My hope is in thee.

For centuries the writ of empiricism has been spreading into the ancient domain of transcendentalist belief, slowly at the start but quickening in the scientific age. The spirits our ancestors knew intimately first fled the rocks and trees, then the distant mountains. Now they are in the stars, where their final extinction is possible. *But we cannot live without them.* People need a sacred narrative. In one form or other, however intellectualized, they must have a sense of larger purpose. They will refuse to yield to the despair of animal mortality. They will continue to plead in company with the psalmist, *Now Lord, what is my comfort?* They will find a way to keep the ancestral spirits alive.

If the sacred narrative cannot be in the form of a religious cosmology, it will be taken from the material history of the universe and the human species.

That trend is in no way debasing. The true evolutionary epic, retold as poetry, is as intrinsically ennobling as any religious epic. Material reality discovered by science already possesses more content and grandeur than all religious cosmologies combined. The continuity of the human line has been traced through a period of deep history a thousand times older than that conceived by the Western religions. Its study has brought new revelations of great moral importance. It has made us realize that *Homo sapiens* is far more than a congeries of tribes and races. We are a single gene pool from which individuals are drawn in each generation and into which they are dissolved the next generation, forever united as a species by heritage and a common future. Such are the conceptions, based on fact, from which new intimations of immortality can be drawn and a new mythos evolved.

Which world-view prevails, religious transcendentalism or scientific empiricism, will make a great difference in the way humanity claims the future. During the time the matter is under advisement, an accommodation can be reached if the following overriding fact is realized. On the one side ethics and religion are still too complex for present-day science to explain in depth. On the other they are far more a product of autonomous evolution than hitherto conceded by most theologians. Science faces in ethics and religion its most interesting and possibly humbling challenge, while religion must somehow find the way to incorporate the discoveries of science in order to retain credibility. Religion will possess strength to the extent that it codifies and puts into enduring, poetic form the highest values of humanity consistent with empirical knowledge; that is the only way to provide compelling moral leadership. Blind faith no matter how passionately expressed will not suffice. Science for its part will test restlessly every assumption about the human condition and in time uncover the bedrock of the moral and religious sentiments.

The eventual result of the competition between the two world-views, I believe, will be the secularization of the human epic and of religion itself. However the process plays out, it demands unwavering intellectual rigor in an atmosphere of mutual respect.

Notes
on the Contributors

BEN BIRNBAUM is the editor of *Boston College Magazine*. His poems and essays have appeared in *Image*, among other journals, and in *The Best American Essays 2001*. He once shoveled camel droppings for a circus in Australia and was a cab driver in Brooklyn. Editing a magazine pales by comparison.

ANNIE CALLAN is the author of *Taf* (a novel), *Migrations* (a play), and *The Back Door* (poems). She teaches at the Northwest Writing Institute at Lewis and Clark College in Portland. Annie can remember vast snatches of poetry and recites them at the drop of a hat without the slightest hitch in her voice. It's an amazing thing altogether, definitely.

JOHN DANIEL, winner of two Oregon Book Awards, is the author of *Looking After* (a memoir of his mother), *The Trail Home* (essays), and two books of poems. His newest book is a memoir, *Winter Creek*, which is in part about the land where he and his wife, Marilyn, live in Elmira, Oregon. He is the tallest of the contributors to this volume.

BRIAN DOYLE is the editor of *Portland Magazine* at the University of Portland. He is the author of two essay collections, *Saints Passionate & Peculiar* and *Credo*, and co-author, with his father Jim

Doyle, of *Two Voices*, a collection of their essays. Brian's essays have appeared in *Best American Essays 1998* and *1999*.

ANDRE DUBUS, who died in 1999, was the author of seven collections of stories, a novel *(The Lieutenant)*, and two collections of essays, *Broken Vessels* and *Meditations from a Movable Chair*. His phone calls twice a year were for eight years a source of great entertainment for the editor of *Portland Magazine*. God rest his sweet brawling drawling soul.

DAVID JAMES DUNCAN is a skinny Scottish-American flyfisherman who drinks only Scotch whiskey, the poor burro. He is the author of two novels, *The River Why* and *The Brothers K*, and two collections of essays, *River Teeth* and *My Story as Told by Water*. He lives in Lolo, Montana, and is, with Ian Frazier, *Portland Magazine*'s Piscine Editorial Board.

MARY GORDON is the author of many novels, most recently *Spending*, and of several works of nonfiction, most recently a memoir of her father, *Shadow Man*. She is a professor of literature and writing at Barnard College and lives in New York City.

TONY HILLERMAN, whose "Navajo detective novels" are savored the world over, is the author of fifteen novels, several collections of essays, and a memoir, *Seldom Disappointed*, from which this excerpt was drawn. For many years a newspaper reporter and editor, and then, poor lamb, a journalism professor and advisor to a university president, he is married to Marie, one of the coolest women you'll ever meet.

BARRY LOPEZ is the author of many books of fiction and nonfiction, among them *Arctic Dreams*, which won the National Book Award in 1986, and *Light Action in the Caribbean*, his most recent collection of stories. He lives in Oregon and advises the editor of *Portland Magazine* in basketball and vocabularic matters.

MELISSA MADENSKI is an essayist, poet, and author of two books for children, *Some of the Pieces* and *In My Mother's Garden*. She lives on the Oregon coast and is *Portland Magazine*'s consulting editor on matters having to do with creeks and streams.

LOUIS MASSON is a professor of literature and writing at the University of Portland. He is the author of *Reflections*, a collection of essays. He is *Portland Magazine*'s one and only contributing editor.

GREG MCNAMEE of Tucson, Arizona, is the author, editor, or translator of ten books, among them *The Sierra Club Book of Deserts* and (with the great photographer Art Wolfe) *In the Presence of Wolves*.

KATHLEEN DEAN MOORE is a professor of philosophy at Oregon State University in Corvallis, Oregon, and the author of the essay collections *Riverwalking* and *Holdfast*. Her essay here is from *Holdfast*.

CYNTHIA OZICK is the author of several novels, notably *The Shawl* and *The Puttermesser Papers*, and of several collections of essays. She lives in New Rochelle, New York. She is *Portland Magazine*'s correspondent in Matters Judaical and Biblical.

CHET RAYMO, professor of physics at Stonehill College in Massachusetts, is a science columnist for the Boston Globe and the author of many books, most recently *The Path: A One-Mile Walk to Environmental Awareness*.

PATTIANN ROGERS is the author of eight books of poetry, most recently *Song of the World Becoming* (her collected poems) and of a prose book about poetry, *The Song of the Marsh Wren*, which is really good. She and her husband, John, live in Castle Rock, Colorado. Pattiann is *Portland Magazine*'s Consulting Editor on All Matters Poetical.

MARY LEE SETTLE is a novelist most famously of the pile of novels called collectively the Beulah Quintet. She is also the author of *All the Little Live Things*, a memoir of her service in England during the Second World War. She lives in Virginia.

MOST REVEREND WILLIAM SKYLSTAD is the bishop of Spokane, Washington. He was the driving force of the first international pastoral letter in North America, on the holiness of the Columbia River.

KIM STAFFORD is the director of the Northwest Writing Institute at Lewis and Clark College in Portland, the author of many books of poetry (the most recent being *A Thousand Friends of Rain*) and author of several works of nonfiction, notably the excellent essay collection *Having Everything Right*. Stafford is *Portland Magazine*'s ale editor.

MARGARET O'BRIEN STEINFELS, editor of *Commonweal* magazine since 1989, is the author of *Who's Minding the Children: The History and Politics of Day Care in America*, and former editor of both *Church* magazine and *Christianity & Crisis* magazine. She lives in New York City.

SALLIE TISDALE is the author of many books, among them *Stepping Westward*, about the character of the Pacific Northwest, and *Lot's Wife*, about the lore and science of salt. She lives in Portland.

MARGARET VISSER is a Canadian writer who now lives in Spain. She is the author of *Much Depends on Dinner*, *The Rituals of Dinner*, and *The Way We Are*; her essay is drawn from *The Geometry of Love: Space, Time, Mystery, and Meaning in an Ordinary Church*.

MOST REVEREND JOHN VLAZNY is the archbishop of Portland, Oregon, and an able essayist for *The Catholic Sentinel* newspaper in Oregon. He is *Portland Magazine*'s consulting editor on matters having to do with Chicago, canon law, or both.

TERRY TEMPEST WILLIAMS is the author of many books, among them the classic *Refuge* and most recently a collection of essays and talks called *Red*. She and her husband, Brooke, live in rural Utah. Terry is also an advisor on professional basketball and avian matters for *Portland Magazine*.

EDWARD O. WILSON, professor emeritus of biology at Harvard University, is perhaps the preeminent biologist in the world, and the author of many books, among them *Consilience*, from which this essay was adapted.

Grateful acknowledgment is made to the following for permission to reprint copyrighted material:

"I would like my love to die" from *Collected Poems in English and French* by Samuel Beckett, (New York: Grove Press, 1977), p. 61.

"Why I Pray" reprinted by permission of the author, copyright © Ben Birnbaum.

"The Ambulance Prayer" reprinted by permission of the author, copyright © Annie Callan.

"Holy Waters" reprinted by permission of the author, copyright © John Daniel.

"Leap" reprinted by permission of the author, copyright © Brian Doyle.

"Making Sandwiches for My Daughters" reprinted by permission of the estate of Andre Dubus, copyright © Andre Dubus.

"Gladly" reprinted by permission of the author, copyright © David James Duncan.

"Six Prayers" reprinted by permission of the author, copyright © Mary Gordon.

"Offer It Up" from *Seldom Disappointed*, reprinted by permission of the author, copyright © Tony Hillerman.

"God's Love on a Darkling Plain" reprinted by permission of the author, copyright © 1997 Barry Holstun Lopez.

"Breathless" reprinted by permission of the author, copyright © Melissa Madenski.

"Holy Places, Holy People" reprinted by permission of the author, copyright © Louis Masson.

"Spiritual Peaks" reprinted by permission of the author, copyright © Gregory McNamee.

"Baking Bread with My Daughter" reprinted by permission of the author, copyright © Kathleen Dean Moore.

"Love Is What We Do" reprinted by permission of the author, copyright © Cynthia Ozick.

"Rain" and "Where God's Grief Appears" reprinted by permission of the author, copyright © Pattiann Rogers.

OTHER RESOURCES FROM AUGSBURG

Kindred Sisters by Dandi Daley Mackall
160 pages, 0-8066-2828-6

An insightful book about the connections between the lives
and faith of women of the New Testament and comtemporary
women of all ages. Ideal for either personal reflection or group
study.

The Magdalene Gospel by Mary Ellen Ashcroft
144 pages, 0-8066-4358-7

Drawing on creative imagination and contemporary scripture
scholarship, Mary Ellen Ashcroft lets the women of the gospel
speak for themselves. Each woman "comes to life" and shares her
own story of liberating grace and loving encounter with Jesus.

A Joyful Theology by Sara Maitland
144 pages, 0-8066-4473-7

A lively exploration of creation to learn more about the Creator.
The author finds a God who inspires awe, who calls us to be
committed to one another, and who invites us to live in joy.

Of Earth and Sky by Thomas Becknell
160 pages, 0-8066-4260-2

A combination of classic and contemporary selections from
more than eighty of the world's finest writers to illustrate the
seven virtues as they are taught through nature. Accompanied
by beautiful, simple drawings, these selections encourage personal contemplation, enriching the spiritual life.

Available wherever books are sold.
To order these books directly, contact:
1-800-328-4648 • www.augsburgbooks.com
Augsburg Fortress, Publishers
P.O. Box 1209, Minneapolis, MN 55440-1209